The story of Loganair

Scotland's Airline — The first 25 years

Iain Hutchison

Published by Western Isles Publishing Co Ltd
Phototypeset by Essprint Ltd
Printed by Nevisprint Ltd

ISBN 0 906437 14 8

Acknowledgments

Sincere thanks must be expressed in appreciation of the assistance given by a large number of people. Many have given me not only enthusiastic access to their knowledge but have also made their time freely available and have extended the hospitality of their homes. I am truly grateful for their support.

I would particularly like to thank Captain Ken Foster, formerly Operations Director of Loganair, who spent twenty years with the company from 1963 until 1983. Captain Foster kindly made himself available for various sessions and without these it would have been exceedingly difficult to compile the historical sections of this book.

Additionally I would like to extend my thanks to Loganair's Managing Director, Scott Grier, who provided much useful assistance, advice and encouragement. He also arranged access to much historical material retained in the company's archives — a unique collection of press cuttings and other documents which give many insights to the airline's development.

I would also like to convey special thanks to the following:
Captain Jamie Bayley (Shorts 360 Fleet Manager, Loganair, Glasgow)
Gil Fraser (Engineering Manager, Loganair, Glasgow)
Ian Harper (son-in-law of the late Captain David Barclay MBE OStJ)
Archie MacArthur (Station Manager, Loganair, Tiree)
Captain Duncan McIntosh (Founder & Managing Director, Loganair until 1982)
Hamish McKean (Customer Services Manager, Loganair)
Maisie Muir (Royal Bank of Scotland, Kirkwall)
Bill Palmer (formerly Northern & Scottish Airways and BEA)
Ivor Robertson (Marketing Manager, Loganair)
Morag Sinclair (Castlebay, Isle of Barra)
Captain Eric Starling (formerly Allied Airways, Scottish Airways and BEA)
Gisela Thürauf (Nursing Officer, Southern General Hospital, Glasgow)
Captain Alan Whitfield (formerly Loganair Senior Pilot, Shetland)

Lastly I would like to say a special 'thank you' to Chuti, Panee and Narin for their patience with me during the months when this project became a growing obsession.

Glasgow, January 1987   Iain C Hutchison

2

Contents

Roimh-ràdh

Tha e nis leth-cheud bliadhna bhon a thòisich muinntir na Gàidhealtachd agus na h-Eileanan a dhol air iteig airson tursan eadar-dhealaichte chun nam bailtean mòra. Bha luchd-turais a' smaointinn bho thùs gu robh iad a' faotainn seallaidh alainn air na h-eileanan bho bhàta aiseig biodh i bho shiùil, smùid no ola; ach cha ghabh seo a bhith air a choimeas an-diugh nuair a thèid duine air iteig ann am pleuna air latha brèagha. Tha daoine nis a' gabhail don phleun gun smaointeachadh; caigeann bhliadhnaichean air ais bhiodh an cridhe nam beul leis an eagal gus an ruigeadh iad an ceann-uidhe agus am beanadh na rothan air an raon-laighe.

Se cosgais an t-slighe an gearain as motha tha aig a' mhòr chuid an aghaidh a dhol air itealan. Tha e ri fhaicinn gu bheil an Riaghaltas agus na h-Ughdarasan Ionadail a' toirt cuideachadh mòran airgid do ghoireasan-siubhail de gach seòrsa, ach am bitheantas feumaidh luchd nam pleunaichean a bhith strì gu làidir le gainne airgid a chumail nan seirbhisean aca dol. Cò aig tha fhios nan robh am barrachd cuideachadh airgid air a thoirt do na pleunaichean nach bitheadh luchd siubhail nan eilean a mhàin a' seachnadh nam bàtaichean aiseig agus a' dol air iteig.

Se iomradh san fharsaingeachd a tha san leabhar seo air na h-itealain a bha, 'sa tha anns a' Ghàidhealtachd, ach tha mion-chùnntas air a thoirt air Loganair a thaobh an luchd obrach, sligheachan adhair, pleunaichean cumanta agus pleunaichean eiridinn. A' bruidhinn air an fheadhainn mu dheireadh — 's iomadh beatha bha air a sàbhaladh anns na h-eileanan nuair a chaidh daoine fìor thinn a ghiùlan gu ospadal air tir mòr.

Nuair a chuimhnicheas sinn air pleunaichean-eiridinn tha ainm Sìne Cheanadach (a' bhanaltram a bhuineadh do eilean Cholla a chaill a beatha ann an tubaist pleuna air eilean Ile) a' tighinn gu inntinn a h-uile duine. Ged nach biodh adhbhar sam bith eile aig an leabhar seo ach a bhith na chuimhneachan air Sìne agus a' toirt taing do na sgiobairean-adhair agus na banaltraim a tha gus an latha an-diugh a' cur am beatha ann an cunnart anns na pleunaichean eiridinn airson daoine tinn a shabhaladh — nach bu mhath an t-ùmhlachd e.

Eilean Thiriodh   Ailig MacArtair

4

Introduction

The nineteen-thirties saw the golden age of the pioneers of Scottish civil aviation. Although some of the early companies were to enjoy only a short existence their names and those of the far-sighted men who were behind them are well remembered half a century later.

In the north, Highland Airways pioneered services from their base at Inverness to the Orkney and Shetland Islands, while Aberdeen Airways, later renamed Allied Airways, provided spirited competition on these northern routes from their base at Dyce. In the west, Midland and Scottish Air Ferries pioneered routes from Renfrew to Campbeltown, Islay and Belfast. Following their demise, Northern and Scottish Airways took up their lead and added services to Skye, North Uist, Benbecula, South Uist, Barra, and latterly Stornoway on Lewis.

Then came the Second World War in 1939 and much of the development work of these airlines came to a halt for the next five years. Aircraft, with windows blacked out, did continue to operate very restricted scheduled and air ambulance flights from 1939 until 1945. After the war it looked at first as if things were to carry on much as before, but in 1947 all the private airlines were nationalised. Under the new British European Airways Corporation a pattern of services was resumed on the main routes, but the nature of these remained fairly static over many years.

When Loganair arrived on the scene in 1962 as a fledgling operator there were many gaps in aviation services which the state airline would not or could not fill but which were nonetheless beckoning. Loganair has been seen to pursue these opportunities in the full spirit of the earlier pioneers. That it has been no less successful may be observed from the present stature of the airline. The work of these new pioneers has also been acknowledged in the award of the OBE to Captain Duncan McIntosh, founder of the airline, for his services to the communities of the Highlands and Islands, and in the award of the Queen's Commendation for valuable services in the air to Captain Ken Foster, formerly Operations Director, and to Captain Alan Whitfield, formerly senior pilot in Shetland.

Written from the outside looking in, this small book seeks to provide an insight into the growth and operations of a unique airline. There are no doubt many more stories to be told which may perhaps be revealed one day in a personal account by one of those who have been on the inside and 'in the thick of it'.

Piper Aztec G-ASER   *Photo by courtesy of Captain Duncan McIntosh*

The Loganair fleet at Renfrew in 1964 — Piper Cherokee 180, Piper Tripacer, Piper Aztecs
Photo by courtesy of Captain Ken Foster

The Logan Era

Loganair came into being on 1st February 1962 when the Logan Construction Co Ltd commenced operation of its own aircraft to fulfil a role previously undertaken by a small air taxi company, Capital Services (Aero) Ltd.

That company had commenced operations during the previous year with Captain Duncan McIntosh flying its sole Piper Apache aircraft on a variety of charter duties. Captain McIntosh had previously been a pilot with the RAF during the Second World War and latterly he had been Chief Test Pilot with the Shoreham-based Miles Aircraft Co. Captain McIntosh, affectionately known as Captain Mac by many colleagues over the years which have since passed, became manager-cum-pilot of Logan's new venture. The Loganair fleet consisted of one Piper Aztec aircraft based at Edinburgh Turnhouse Airport, where Captain McIntosh was also a Flight Commander with No. 603 Squadron RAAF.

The Logan Construction Co Ltd was run by Willie Logan at this time, but the company had originally been established by his father, Duncan Logan, as a small stone-cutting business at Muir of Ord, Ross-shire. By the nineteen-sixties, however, the company had become one of Scotland's foremost construction companies taking on projects such as hydro-electric dams, the Fort William pulp mill and many major road reconstructions.

With the establishment of its aviation division Logan Construction could move both executives and key workers quickly from one site to another in the Piper Aztec PA23A (G-ARMH) which was based at Renfrew Airport as a new operating base at an early stage. The role of Loganair was highlighted in 1963 when Willie Logan made the headlines by flying into Dundee (Riverside Park) with the successful tender for the construction of the Tay Road Bridge only fifteen minutes before the deadline for the submission of tenders for the contract.

The Logan Construction Co Ltd tried hard to win contracts abroad too and the company's aircraft made trips to Scandinavia, Finland, France, Corsica, Spain, Gibraltar and Ireland in pursuit of these, although success failed to match the effort. On the home front flights were frequently made from Renfrew to the company's Muir of Ord offices; and, while work was continuing at the Fort William pulp mill, flights landed at a makeshift strip at Camisky on the Great Glen Cattle Ranch.

During 1963 a second Aztec was added to the fleet, a PA23B (G-ASER) and also a single-engined Piper Tripacer (G-ARHV). The Tripacer was mainly used for aerial photography by the media and by private organisations such as civil engineering firms monitoring progress on their projects. Aerial photographs appearing in the press covered a wide range of topics. On the Clyde the atomic submarine 'Dreadnought' was photographed during trials while the activities of the United States Navy on the Holy Loch were also the subject of much public interest. Further up the Clyde, the Cunard liner 'Queen Elizabeth' was put on film as she was manoeuvred into dry dock in 1965, while on the Firth of Forth dramatic shots of the Forth Road Bridge had been provided as the handsome suspension bridge inched its way towards completion in 1964. Other topics for aerial photography included a crowded Hampden Park football ground and, frequently, the chaos caused by snow-blocked roads under the onslaught of winter.

The second Piper Aztec was used on outside work which started to become available to the company with increasing frequency and Captains Ken Foster and Lynn John joined Loganair in 1963 to do much of the public transport flying. The company was awarded a contract by the Army to take mail, food and other supplies (such as films for the cinema) to the radar station on the remote Atlantic island of St Kilda whose remaining native population had been evacuated in 1930. Operation of the flights was dictated by the vagaries of the weather and the supplies had to be dropped from a very low level onto the main island of Hirta as there was no landing area. Loganair also assisted the Army at the missile range on Benbecula flying for radar calibration.

The Territorial Army also found a use for Loganair's fleet — as target aircraft for their gunners. The gunners were put through a series of graded exercises at places such as Inverness, Stornoway, Kirkwall and Lerwick. Cameras fitted to the guns of the TA enabled examiners to guage the accuracy of the marksmanship — a device obviously preferable to the use of live ammunition.

Useful bread and butter work was provided by Littlewoods Pools with a contract to fly coupons from Renfrew to Belfast from 1963 to 1965, and from Belfast to Liverpool in 1966. In 1968 a contract was awarded by the Post Office Savings Bank to carry computer cards from Glasgow to Blackpool. The computer cards were collected from the POSB offices at Cowglen in Glasgow at the end of the working day and were processed overnight on the Premium Bond computer 'Ernie' at Lytham St Annes. The processed cards were then flown north again to be returned to the desks of the POSB staff at Cowglen before their arrival at work the following morning.

1964 saw the commencement of a contract to carry newspapers from Glasgow to Stornoway enabling morning papers to be available on the Isle of Lewis several hours before the arrival of the BEA scheduled service. Upon arrival at Stornoway the Aztec aircraft would then be available for charter which could entail the aircraft taking businessmen to Edinburgh or Belfast, or perhaps landing on the airstrip at Evanton to let councillors attend a meeting of Ross and Cromarty County Council in Dingwall. The service was a quick way for the islanders to get lobsters to mainland customers and the service was soon carrying a variety of goods. Harris tweeds were also flown out of Stornoway; and with the inclusion of Benbecula into the service the NAAFI there used the flight as a source of fresh milk and vegetables while mail was also carried for the Post Office. The Stornoway newspaper run was to become one of Loganair's success stories operating for ten years without ever being grounded by the worst weather that the West Coast could throw at it.

Loganair was eventually permitted to carry fifteen passengers per week on the return flight from Stornoway to Glasgow following earlier applications successfully opposed by BEA. But this was by no means the airline's first scheduled passenger service; that honour belongs to a route from Dundee to Edinburgh inaugurated in October 1963.

Loganair pioneered Riverside Park at Dundee as an airfield, but that was not an isolated instance. Efforts to promote the idea that main towns should have their own 'airpark' did not have an overwhelming impact, but were nonetheless instrumental in the establishment of airstrips at the new towns of Glenrothes and Cumbernauld.

Further north a wartime airfield at North Connel was resuscitated while a new airstrip was constructed at Glenforsa on the Isle of Mull by the Royal Engineers under the OPMAC (Operation Military Aid to the Community) scheme. This led to a Glasgow—Oban—Mull scheduled service commencing in 1966.

An airstrip was laid out on the Highland Showground at Muir of Ord for the flights to the northern headquarters of the Logan Construction Co Ltd. An airstrip was also laid out by the group at Aultbea for the duration of a three million pound construction contract for NATO. A Piper Cherokee 180 had been purchased for the Aultbea operation and with the aircraft came a pair of floats, but with the new airstrip it was never necessary to utilise them.

This three-passenger aircraft was later replaced by a Piper Cherokee 6 which could carry five passengers. Duties allocated to it included the ferrying of positioning crews of other carriers, such as Scandinavian Airlines, from Prestwick to Renfrew, and the transferring of businessmen alighting from trans-Atlantic flights at Prestwick to Glenrothes or Cumbernauld. The Cherokee 6 was also a popular aircraft for aerial photography.

In 1963 Loganair established the Glasgow Flying Club although it withdrew from this interest in later years as it became more involved in the mainstream of civil aviation. Captain McIntosh also brought the Miles Student jet trainer to Scotland. Plans to open a school to train jet pilots did not come to fruition even although such an establishment would have been the first of its kind in the UK. The Miles Student, in storage at the Loganair hangar at Glasgow until April 1983, remained a source of interest to aviation enthusiasts.

In 1965 Loganair was pursuing plans for new scheduled services and was having discussions with Britten-Norman Ltd which was developing plans for its Islander aircraft. Tragedy then struck Loganair's parent company twice in rapid succession.

Willie Logan broke a lifetime rule of his forbidding Sunday work in order to supervise lifting operations at the Tay Road Bridge on Sunday 12th December. During the course of this a jib fell from the Bridge and he sustained a cracked collarbone and a hand injury while three men lost their lives in the accident.

One month later the second and greater tragedy occurred. Willie Logan wished to fly from Edinburgh to Inverness on Saturday 23rd January 1966. Loganair's own fleet was fully committed so he chartered a Piper Aztec from Auchterarder-based Strathallan Air Services Ltd. The aircraft crashed into the slopes of Craig Dunain on its approach to Inverness and although the pilot survived Willie Logan was killed instantly.

Loganair became a limited company in 1966 and work for the Logan Construction Co Ltd was now becoming a decreasing part of its overall activities. Plans were being made to revive the Orkneys internal air service, last operated in the nineteen-thirties by Highland Airways, and the development of the Islander aircraft was to be crucial to this operation.

Loganair took delivery of the first production Islander (G-ATWU) in July 1967, but this had to be on a short leasing arrangement for crew training and route trials and then it had to be returned to Britten-Norman because of the loss of their prototype. The aircraft was flown at the Farnborough Air Show that year by Captain McIntosh and at the Prestwick Air Show by Captain Geoff Rosenbloom. There was already great anticipation when the replacement model, fourth off the production line (G-AVKC), arrived in August 1967 then to be taken north to the Orkneys by Captain Jim Lee to inaugurate the internal air service.

On Tuesday 8th October 1968 the share capital of Loganair Ltd was acquired by the National Commercial Bank of Scotland. The National Commercial Bank merged with the Royal Bank of Scotland in the following year. In 1975 the well known name of Logan Construction Co Ltd was later to disappear from the Scottish building scene following cash flow difficulties which arose during the erection of Glasgow's Kingston Bridge for which it was one of the main contractors.

Above **Beech E18S and** *below* **Shorts Skyvan both at Glasgow in 1974**   *Photos by Stuart G Sim*

An Airline to Bank On (1968-1983)

On the takeover, the National Commercial Bank of Scotland's General Manager, Mr J G Robertson, became Chairman of Loganair Ltd. With over four hundred branches nationwide the bank could indeed envisage the airline as having a part to play in their internal communications, but that was entirely secondary to their view of Loganair Ltd as a growing enterprise which could produce profits.

Nor did the bank in any way regard the ownership of a small airline as being incompatible with their banking activities. They had already been innovators in the banking field, establishing the first mobile bank in 1946 on the Isle of Lewis. Having taken to the road in the Western Isles, they then took to the high seas and the northern isles of Orkney in 1962 with the introduction of the boat bank, or Otter Bank. Taking to the air in 1968 must have seemed a natural progression.

Later Mr John B Burke, then Managing Director of the Royal Bank of Scotland, became Chairman of Loganair Ltd. Captain McIntosh was Managing Director. As the airline grew in the nineteen-seventies the Board was expanded to include a team of working directors. Captain Ken Foster was appointed as Flight Operations Director, Mr Gil Fraser as Engineering Director and Mr Scott Grier as Financial Director. Mr Burke was tragically killed in a climbing accident in November 1983. Mr. Charles Winter then served as Chairman for the few remaining days of the Royal Bank of Scotland's ownership of Loganair Ltd.

At the time of the takeover by the National Commercial Bank of Scotland, the first Britten-Norman Islanders had already been delivered and had established themselves as the mainstay of the Loganair fleet.

But within a week of the bank acquiring Loganair another new aircraft, a previously ordered Beech E18S (G-ASUG), arrived and was added to the Loganair pool of aircraft. G-ASUG, however, was not the aircraft that had originally been sought when this aircraft type was evaluated. Three Beech 18s (C-45s), in immaculate condition, were purchased from the Royal Canadian Air Force at Prestwick. It was planned that these aircraft would form the nucleus of the fleet which would be employed in the development of the Loganair scheduled network.

However these particular aircraft had not been assembled in the USA by their American manufacturers, but had arrived in Canada by road for assembly there. The result was that their existence proved difficult to establish in the eyes of the British authorities since their country of manufacture was the USA, but the aircraft had never been registered there. This anomaly presented a major obstacle in establishing the aircraft on the UK register and finally one of the aircraft was sold while dismantling for parts was the fate of the other two.

G-ASUG was acquired from BKS Ltd with whom it had been employed as an aerial survey aircraft. As this was the first Beech 18 on the British Register, the aircraft still had to go through a full flight certification programme before a Certificate of Airworthiness could be granted to allow its use as a public transport aeroplane. This was carried out at Prestwick by Scottish Aviation Ltd with Captain McIntosh performing many of the test flights. The aircraft then went on to perform faithfully as workhorse on the Stornoway service, served on the Glasgow—Aberdeen—Stavanger scheduled service, and with its comforts and long range capability was a popular aircraft for executive charters. It was retired in 1975 having flown for twenty-two years and may now be viewed at the Museum of Flight at East Fortune where it is preserved.

The Royal Bank of Scotland became the 'high street' bank of the National Commercial banking group and it rapidly became useful for Loganair to have the Royal Bank behind it because of the strength and stability which it epitomised. From the bank there was a realisation of the goodwill that could be created through its involvement in a third level airline whose routes in many areas were to become important socially. In order to show that the airline was being encouraged to think to the future and in preparation for an anticipated BEA rationalisation, an order for a Shorts Skyvan 3 was placed on 14th October 1968.

The Shorts Skyvan 3, G-AWYG, was delivered on 3rd March 1969, the first of the type to a British operator. With a payload of up to eighteen passengers or 4,000 pounds of cargo, it was much larger than any previous Loganair aircraft. Its primary use was on the Stornoway and Stavanger routes. The functional box shape allowed it to carry both bulky and heavy cargoes and in this it was often in a class of its own. However, abnormal cargo loads did not arise frequently enough to permit adequate utilisation of its unique carrying capability. It was an expensive aircraft to operate and fuel loadings for longer journeys often restricted the payload to between twelve and fifteen passengers and their baggage. After five years' service it was phased out of the fleet and sold to a US operator.

With the dawning of the seventies new scheduled services were inaugurated. A feeder service from Dundee to Glasgow was launched from Leuchars until sufficient improvements had been made to the airfield at Riverside Park for it to be licensed; the service relocated there in 1971. Riverside Park is only one mile from the city centre and so was much more convenient to the majority of travellers.

Following the success of the Orkney inter-island services, airfields were being developed in Shetland, but, unlike Orkney, the concept of internal air services was entirely new to Shetland. Initially the service was limited to a route from Sumburgh to the northernmost island, Unst. Gradually the network of airstrips was expanded and perhaps the most important innovation was the building of airstrips on islands whose population could not support scheduled services, but whose continued existences as places of human habitation were to some extent safeguarded by the introduction of charter and air ambulance flights. The development of the airfield at Tingwall, close to Lerwick, was also important in bringing about an integrated inter-island air network.

The completion of Breakish airstrip on the Isle of Skye, by Army engineers newly returned from Far Eastern postings undertaking this project as part of the OPMAC scheme, saw the launching of new scheduled services immediately. These linked Eilean a' Cheo (The Misty Isle) with both Glasgow and Inverness.

The award of the contract to operate the Scottish Air Ambulance Service by the Scottish Home and Health Department in 1973 made Loganair's gamut of operations three-pronged by adding this service to its charter and scheduled services. While Loganair had in fact been operating air ambulance flights since 1967 in a supplementary role to that of BEA, the award of the full contract was a fitting acknowledgment of the expertise which the airline had built up during the first decade of its existence.

Loganair was given cause for concern when in 1971 Britten-Norman, the manufacturer of the Islander aircraft, went into receivership. This could have had serious implications for Loganair as the Islanders were now performing an important role for the airline and the features of this rugged aircraft were unique to the manufacturer. Fortunately the Britten-Norman operation was acquired by the Fairey Group and production continued at Gosselies in Belgium. (In 1977 the Fairey Group was taken over by Pilatus of Switzerland.)

The crisis over, Loganair was ready to make another advance in which Britten-Norman was to play an important role. This was the ordering of the Trislander aircraft in 1973. The Trislander is effectively a stretched version of the Islander, carrying sixteen passengers with two pilots and with a third engine, from which it takes its name, mounted high in the tail. The first Trislander to be delivered to Loganair, G-BAXD, was only the tenth production model and was the first to come off the assembly line at Gosselies.

The Trislanders arrived in a new colour scheme that was gradually being applied to the existing fleet. The previous thin bands of red and black on a white fuselage were replaced with a distinctive red band while the underside of the aircraft was painted black. The black belly of the aircraft proved to be a useful camouflage for the mud and the livestock droppings (referred to as 'sharn' in Orkney) which became splattered across the aircraft fuselage when operating to some of the more basic aerodromes.

G-BAXD was quickly joined by a further two Trislanders and this permitted the disposal of the Skyvan and retiral of the Beech 18. The Beech 18 had been refurbished for executive charter work, carrying seven passengers in comfort, but it had become increasingly difficult and costly to maintain.

Further scheduled service developments took place when Loganair's Trislanders commenced operating on behalf of British Airways (which now incorporated the old BEA) on the Glasgow—Tiree—Barra service in September 1974. Loganair took over operation of this service in its own right in the following spring. Other services developed following the publication of the Civil Aviation Authority's report 'Air Transport in the Scottish Highlands and Islands' of 1974 which highlighted the value of third level feeder services and in 1976 Loganair took over the Inverness—Wick—Kirkwall route from British Airways. This was followed by the British Airways services from Glasgow to Campbeltown and Islay on 1st April 1977.

By 1976 the fleet consisted of eight Islanders and six Trislanders, the latest Trislanders (Series 2) having an extended baggage compartment in the nose from which they earned the nickname "Snoopy". By this time the fleet was sporting the new stylised logo on the fin, the creation of Glasgow-based Randak Designs. The logo is intended to be symbolic of the mountains and glens which form so much of the terrain over which the airline flies.

The first of another aircraft type arrived in 1977 with the delivery of the Canadian-built DHC-6-310 Twin Otter. The aircraft had been ordered to serve the growing North Sea oil industry and at half-a-million pounds was the most expensive acquisition yet by Loganair. The aircraft was an immediate success on oil-related flights with its high

**Britten-Norman
Trislander Series 1
Isle of Skye, 1974**

**Britten-Norman
Trislander Series 2
Glasgow, 1978**

**Embraer Bandeirante
Glasgow, 1983**

Photos by the author

Shorts 330 in flight *Photo by courtesy of Captain Ken Foster*

degree of passenger comfort and STOL (Short Take-Off and Landing) performance. The Twin Otters became the mainstay of the company's oil support fleet with seven of the type based at Aberdeen and they were supported by three Trislanders (Series 1).

The three Trislanders (Series 2) were taking on the important role of workhorses on the denser scheduled routes, but additional Twin Otters were soon introduced to scheduled service work, inaugurating new routes from Edinburgh to Lerwick (Tingwall) and from Glasgow to Londonderry. The introduction of the Twin Otter was partly prompted by the loss of the Chevron oil support contract leaving Loganair with a surplus of this aircraft type. But the Twin Otter, which allowed for the provision of a cabin attendant, was an immediate success with scheduled passengers to the extent that by 1983 they had entirely replaced the Trislanders.

The Twin Otter in its turn was soon upstaged by another aircraft, the thirty-passenger Belfast-built Shorts 330. On this occasion, however, it was not the oil industry that was calling the tune for the Shorts 330 went straight onto scheduled services. Its prime function was to operate the newly introduced Translink service on behalf of the Scottish Airports division of the British Airports Authority carrying trans-Atlantic passengers from Aberdeen and Edinburgh to Prestwick.

The Translink service was started in 1979, but by the following year the Shorts 330 was also serving on further new routes. These were from Edinburgh to Belfast and from Edinburgh to Kirkwall, with the airline now moving up-market to second level operations. The purchase of two Shorts 330 aircraft plus a full inventory of spare components, cost two-and-a-half million pounds.

Further diversification of the Loganair fleet took place in 1980 when the Brazilian-built Embraer Bandeirantes were delivered. The foremost features of this eighteen-passenger aircraft were its range and speed, making it ideally suited to many of the requirements of the oil companies. It was therefore in oil support work that the two Bandeirantes were mainly utilised although they were employed on scheduled services from time to time. But the aircraft did serve on the Glasgow—Belfast and Edinburgh—Inverness routes in 1984 before being withdrawn from the Loganair fleet and put up for sale as a result of the changing needs of the oil industry in fixed wing transportation.

Loganair made another dramatic aircraft order in 1980. This was the four-engined STOL aircraft, the DHC Dash 7. Seating fifty passengers and costing £3 million with spares, it would have been a major step in Loganair's history at that time. It was intended that the Dash 7 would operate between Aberdeen and Unst under contract to Chevron Oil. However, the contract was awarded to Brymon Airways and Loganair did not take delivery of their intended machine.

In the field of scheduled services Loganair had already widened its traditional Scottish operation with the development of services to Northern Ireland. The first real inroads into the English market were made in October 1982 with the taking over of the Edinburgh—Manchester route from British Airways. This route was initially operated by the Shorts 330.

Further development on the Shorts 330 concept by the manufacturers at their Belfast factory saw the arrival of the Shorts 360. Loganair initially ordered one of these thirty-six-passenger aircraft which joined the fleet in 1983 replacing one of the Shorts 330s. The trade up from the 330 to the 360 was completed the following year when a second Shorts 360 was delivered.

In December 1982 Captain Duncan McIntosh retired from Loganair after a twenty-one year career in which he had seen the company grow from a one aircraft one man operation to an airline reaching every corner of Scotland and many points beyond. In 1976 Captain McIntosh was awarded the OBE in recognition of his services to the people of the Highlands and Islands of Scotland. Upon Captain McIntosh's retiral Financial Director Mr Scott Grier was appointed Managing Director.

In 1980/81 the airline had recorded a loss of seven hundred thousand pounds and this was followed by further losses of a million in 1981/82 and three hundred and fifty thousand in 1982/83. These losses reflected the heavy financial burden imposed by the upgrading of the fleet of aircraft; the 1981/82 deficit reflected too the loss of the large Chevron oil support contract which had utilised several Twin Otters.

On 2nd December 1983 the Royal Bank of Scotland sold Loganair Ltd to British Midland Airways, but with Mr Scott Grier acquiring a twenty-five per cent shareholding in the company which he continues to lead as Managing Director. Despite the financial difficulties encountered towards the end of its fifteen year period as a subsidiary of the bank, Loganair Ltd was by no means thereby unique within the aviation industry which is the subject of constant and frequently traumatic change. Indeed, since the bank's first involvement in 1968, the company had grown from a small air taxi operation to become a well-respected regional airline. Its latest addition, only a month before the takeover, was a Fokker Friendship, G-IOMA, leased from British Midland for service on the Edinburgh—Manchester trunk route.

Thus, in December 1983 the Loganair fleet consisted of the following aircraft types:—

1 Fokker Friendship 100	2 Embraer Bandeirante 110
1 Shorts 360	5 DHC-6 Twin Otter
1 Shorts 330	6 Britten-Norman BN-2A Islander

Scheduled Services

Today Loganair serves more destinations in the United Kingdom than any other airline with a comprehensive network that not only covers almost the whole of Scotland, as you would expect of Scotland's airline, but also extends to points in England and Northern Ireland in the form of important trunk routes. But Loganair's first faltering steps into the realm of scheduled services took place in what was only the second year of operation of the original air taxi organisation.

The route was from Riverside Park, Dundee to Edinburgh (Turnhouse) using a five-passenger Piper Aztec. This initial diversification into scheduled passenger flights came about almost by accident as the prime role of Loganair in those early days was to provide transport for the personnel of the Logan Construction Co Ltd. In this role members of the workforce were being carried frequently from Edinburgh to Dundee in connection with the Tay Road Bridge contract when it was discovered that there was a certain demand for similar flights from other businessmen and travellers. The demand was particularly high from passengers wishing to travel from Edinburgh to London, but who were first faced with a circuitous road journey from Dundee to Turnhouse lasting two and three-quarter hours and involving two ferry crossings. The flight took only fifteen minutes and the initial single fare was thirty shillings. However, the demand for the flights was sometimes more apparent than real and therefore their operation was perhaps a little erratic. With the completion of the Forth Road Bridge and in the absence of a big airline infrastructure to promote the service, the service ceased in 1964.

Before the demise of the Dundee—Edinburgh service, plans were already afoot to launch another scheduled service. As early as February 1964 Loganair was evaluating a route linking Renfrew with Oban and Mull; the journey to Mull was taking eight hours by surface transport. Prior to commencing a service, however, an airfield on Mull had to be established and the existing aerodrome at North Connel had to be acquired from the Ministry of Public Buildings and Works by Argyll County Council. The airstrip on Mull was eventually built at Glenforsa in 1966, the first in the West of Scotland to be undertaken by the Royal Engineers under the OPMAC scheme. The project took the Sappers only fifty-four days to complete even although it necessitated the felling of over one thousand trees and the moving of fifty thousand tons of soil. The cost of six thousand pounds was borne by Argyll County Council. Services commenced that year and although the Aztec operated a weekend-only service limited to the summer months, the Glasgow—Oban—Mull service operated initially until 1968.

Loganair wished to make greater use of the aircraft undertaking the Stornoway newspaper service. A passenger service on the return run to Glasgow made sense and there was also a demand for such a flight since the BEA Stornoway—Glasgow service did not take off from Lewis until 1510 and Loganair's early morning flight would leave passengers with a full day in Glasgow or allow onward connections. However, at the Air Transport Licensing Board hearing in December 1965 BEA bitterly opposed the application for a scheduled passenger licence on the grounds that they had lost five million pounds on Highlands and Islands services over the previous eighteen years and each passenger lost to Loganair would further undermine their own service. Even BEA admitted that the needs of the passenger were secondary to their own operational requirements yet the Board turned down Loganair's application. Loganair persevered with their application nonetheless and the first scheduled passengers from Stornoway were using the service in 1966, although they were restricted in number to a maximum of fifteen per week.

The Stornoway—Benbecula—Glasgow service operated for the life of the newspaper run. It was then discontinued in 1974 when British Airways altered their schedules to include a morning flight from Glasgow to Stornoway thereby removing the need for Loganair's special service to fly the newspapers north. It is worth recalling that during its life this service had in fact played a variety of roles. In addition to newspapers being carried to Benbecula and Stornoway, the aircraft uplifted milk at Stornoway for Benbecula which also received fresh vegetables from Glasgow. On its return to Glasgow, in addition to passengers, the aircraft would be carrying Harris tweeds from Stornoway and crabs and lobsters from Benbecula; all of these were just commencing their journeys as exports. Mail was both loaded and unloaded at each point and the pilot was kept busy at each airfield as he restacked his changing cargo.

At the invitation of the Scottish Office in 1964 Loganair applied to mount an inter-island scheduled network in the Orkney Islands. This service was in reality a re-introduction and development of a facility which had been provided by Captain Fresson's Highland Airways until it had been curtailed by the Second World War. New airstrips had to be established throughout the islands, although those on Sanday and North Ronaldsay occupied sites which had been used by Fresson. The initial service, linking Kirkwall, Stronsay, Sanday, North Ronaldsay, Papa Westray and Westray was launched in August 1967 with the delivery of the Britten-Norman Islander aircraft to Loganair, an aircraft type which continues to be ideally suited to this kind of operation. Until 1977 the service was operated coupled with the Orkney Isles Shipping Co Ltd as this enabled government support granted to the shipping company to be available to the air service. For this reason the aircraft operating the Orkney service carried the distinctive logo of the Orkney Isles Shipping Co Ltd, as displayed on the funnels of their vessels, on the tail fin.

In 1971 Eday became the sixth island to be served by flights with the opening of its 'London Airport', named after the nearby Bay of London rather than being an attempt to emulate any other airport with a similar name. Hoy was brought on line in 1973 and Flotta was added on 1st March 1977. The services to the two southern islands, Flotta and Hoy, were discontinued in 1981 with the introduction of a free ferry boat service in Scapa Flow but the northern isles services have enjoyed steady growth since their inception. By July 1972 fifty thousand passengers had used the inter-island services and by September 1975 the one hundred thousandth passenger had been carried. No mean feat for eight passenger aircraft operating on islands with a total population of a mere seventeen thousand. The utilisation of the service is such that the equivalent of the total population of Orkney is transported on the service every year.

Following the success of the Orkney services, the first steps were taken in 1968 to establish a similar network linking the islands of Shetland and the inauguration of a service between Sumburgh and the most northerly island, Unst, where the Royal

Engineers had again been busy in airfield construction under the OPMAC scheme, took place in 1970. A central hub was vital to a Shetland internal operation and the next step was to establish an airfield within close proximity of Lerwick. This resulted in the opening of the first Tingwall aerodrome in 1971. (The present Tingwall Airport was opened in October 1976 to the north of the original airstrip.) Developing the Shetland network involved much self-help in bringing about airfields and Fetlar was added on 25th May 1972, with Whalsay following that autumn. An interruption to services occurred in 1976 when agreement could not be reached with the Shetland Isles Islands Council over a necessary subsidy, but upon the resumption of services Fair Isle was included. The inaugural flight to Fair Isle was flown from Sumburgh on 7th June 1976 in Islander G-AWNR under the command of Captain Ian Ray. With the close proximity of the Sullom Voe oil terminal, Scatsta was also on the scheduled run from July 1978 until October 1979, the first service being flown by Captain M Bray on 25th July in Islander G-AXSS. In 1980 Sumburgh was omitted from the network due to the levying of high charges based on those imposed on flights operating for the oil industry. The Shetland operation was then centred on Lerwick (Tingwall) with the base being transferred there from Sumburgh.

While the Orkney and Shetland operations were the subject of growth, 1969 saw the far-sighted experiment which was not to prove a financial success quickly enough to warrant the start-up costs for what was still a small airline, the Glasgow—Aberdeen—Stavanger route. Had the airline been able to sustain this route it might indeed have yielded great opportunities, but at least for a short time in its early history it was able to refer to its "International Service" and it was a member of IATA (the International Air Transport Association) rubbing shoulders with the big names of world aviation.

In 1970 the airline returned to more familiar ground — Dundee. Since Loganair's brief incursion on its Dundee—Edinburgh route, Dundee had seen other operators, such as British Eagle who had flown from Riverside Park to Renfrew with a De Havilland Dove and Autair International from Leuchars to London with a Hawker Siddeley 748, but the city was again without an air service. This time Loganair decided on Glasgow as a destination using Britten-Norman Islander aircraft for a feeder service from Tayside as there was a wider range of onward services providing greater potential for interlining traffic. This service got off to a slow start as Riverside Park was no longer usable due to water-logging and Leuchars had to be used. When Riverside airfield re-opened in August 1971 passenger loads doubled. The Glasgow—Dundee service quickly became a major route, starting off as a twice daily operation and building up to three times a day. The Shorts Skyvan and Britten-Norman Trislander were also seen on the Dundee—Glasgow route. However the service required subsidy in order to keep fares at an attractive level and when, towards the end of 1975, these were no longer available the service was discontinued.

In 1972 the weekend summer service from Glasgow to Oban and Mull was re-introduced. This time the Islander aircraft continued on to Coll and Tiree and the service was maintained until 1975. With the completion of the airfield at Breakish near Broadford on the Isle of Skye a service from Glasgow was launched. Skye was also linked to Inverness which was the base for other routes to Aberdeen and to Wick via Dornoch.

The Inverness—Dornoch—Wick service was only operated for one season while the Inverness—Skye service was terminated after 1974. The Inverness—Aberdeen route fared a little better and in 1974 incorporated a stop at Kinloss. Dalcross Airport at Inverness was undergoing major runway works at this time and all flights were transferred to Kinloss. Loganair was able to continue flying into Dalcross using a short runway during this period, but included the Kinloss stop to provide an interlining service with British Airways who had been displaced there.

It will be seen that there were several short-lived routes about this period. Indeed many more routes to smaller towns and communities had been under consideration as part of a system of bus stop services operating around the north-east of Scotland, the far north incorporating Easter Ross, Caithness, Sutherland and Wester Ross, and to many of the smaller Hebridean Islands. However 1974 saw aviation everywhere being hit with the full force of the oil crisis with the cost of aircraft fuel multiplying many times over. The result was that many of these rural services would have to operate at much higher fares than had originally been envisaged and their attractiveness to the travelling public would have declined proportionately.

A new service was launched from Inverness in 1975 which was to prove more successful than those to Dornoch, Skye and Aberdeen, and this was a three times daily flight to Edinburgh. The road journey between Inverness and Edinburgh was one of the factors which encouraged travellers to use this service and it was one of the few routes to experience an upturn during the winter rather than the summer. The service operated until 1980 by which time dramatic improvements had been carried out on the A9 Edinburgh—Inverness road. A once daily service was re-introduced in 1984 using a Bandeirante and the service was then operated twice daily by Peregrine Air Services on behalf of Loganair using a Cessna Titan, but this route was again discontinued in early 1985.

1975 also saw the handover of the first of some of British Airways thinner routes with the transfer to Loganair of the services from Glasgow to Tiree and Barra. Loganair also based an aircraft at Stornoway for a new inter-island service linking the Western Isles and on 1st October 1975 Captain J P Knudsen flew Islander G-BANL on the inaugural flight between Stornoway, Benbecula and Barra. Plans to introduce optional stops at points such as Northton (Harris), Berneray and Sollas (North Uist) have not however come to fruition, although at one time the inclusion of Askernish (South Uist) had looked likely.

British Airways' route from Inverness to Wick and Kirkwall was relinquished to Loganair in 1976 and the route's first flight took place on 1st April with Captain Ken Foster and Captain Andy Alsop on the flight deck of Islander G-AXSS. The routes from Glasgow to Campbeltown and Islay followed exactly one year later with Captain Foster flying the inaugural service to Campbeltown in Trislander G-BCYC, while Captain Bill Henley inaugurated the Islay service with sister aircraft G-BDOM. British Airways had served Campbeltown and Islay with one flight a day operated by a Vickers Viscount covering both points — "like using a sledge hammer to crack a nut" to quote one critic of their service. Using Trislanders, Loganair was able to provide a morning flight and an evening flight (and even a midday flight for a period) to both destinations independently which offered greatly improved services and made day return trips in either direction possible. A direct service from Glasgow to Mull was launched in 1978 operating daily, Monday to Saturday, but this attempt at a high frequency service proved no more enduring than the previous services to Mull and it was only operated for two seasons.

A Shorts 330 was acquired to operate the Translink service, under contract to the British Airports Authority, which began in 1979. This linked Aberdeen and Edinburgh with Prestwick with a service designed to connect with trans-Atlantic flights. A service to Prestwick was also operated from Inverness and Belfast with a Twin Otter and this aircraft type was also used on a new non-stop service from Edinburgh to Lerwick. The first flight was operated on 2nd April 1979 by Twin Otter G-RBLA with Captain Alan Whitfield and Captain Jamie Bayley on the flight deck. This service was extended to Unst in 1981. A service from Aberdeen to Lerwick and one from Aberdeen to Stornoway were planned for 1980, but a licence was not granted for the Lerwick service because of strenuous opposition from British Airways and these routes did not materialise. This was the first of three unsuccessful applications for the Aberdeen—Lerwick route with appeals being submitted to the Secretary of State for Trade on two occasions.

The first services out of Scotland since the days of the Norwegian service were operated in 1979 with the launch of two routes. A major route was a newly innovated service between Glasgow and Londonderry which utilised the Twin Otter (the first on scheduled service duties) which was performing the Edinburgh—Lerwick link. The first flight was also flown with Twin Otter G-RBLA on 2nd April 1979. Captain Ken Foster and Captain J Taylor flew the Londonderry-bound service with Captain Whitfield and Captain Bayley flying the return leg. The second route was a summer only weekend service linking Glasgow with Enniskillen which operated for three years. Although this was a Trislander route, Twin Otter G-RBLA was again used for the inaugural service with Captain Foster and Captain R Sullivan at the controls. Another summer only weekend service which operated for four seasons from 1980 was a former Dan-Air route from Prestwick to the Isle of Man. Following the success of the Edinburgh—Lerwick route a similar service from Edinburgh to Kirkwall was established in 1980. In 1981 a stop at Wick was incorporated despite determined opposition from Air Ecosse and by 1984 a Shorts 360 was being used for three out of the six days on which the service operated.

The focus of major expansion, however, continued to be Northern Ireland. From April 1980 Loganair took over the Belfast—Edinburgh route from British Airways and launched the service using the Shorts 330 operating three times daily. That permitted a maximum of 90 passengers a day in either direction and the airline could really be classed as having graduated from third level to second level operations. It was certainly a dramatic contrast for an airline which had so grudgingly been given permission to carry fifteen passengers per week from Stornoway to Glasgow in 1966. In the following year, 1981, a twice daily service was launched from Belfast to Glasgow with the Shorts 330, and from Belfast to Blackpool, the first service to a destination in England. From Londonderry a weekend summer service was commenced in 1983 to both Blackpool and the Isle of Man.

When Loganair first started operating on the Glasgow—Belfast route, they operated a lunch-time service while British Airways operated the peak morning and evening flights. Loganair also operated a 2210 hours departure from Belfast and an 0600 hours departure from Glasgow. Most of the passengers on these unsociably-timed flights were crews who operated British Airways Shuttle flights from Belfast to London and who would not stay overnight in Belfast at that time because of the political unrest there. Loganair went into full competition with British Airways by flying at the peak business times in 1982. Competition with the state airline was not easy and Loganair's big breakthrough came the following year when they persuaded the Shorts Aerospace Company to open their facilities at Sydenham to scheduled flights on 7th February 1983. This new Belfast Harbour Airport is situated in very close proximity of Belfast city centre and has proved immensely popular with the travelling public. Upon transferring its operations from Aldergrove to Belfast Harbour Loganair experienced a forty per cent increase in passenger loads. The new airport was an obvious success and soon all Loganair's Belfast services were switched from Aldergrove.

Loganair had come on to the Glasgow—Inverness route in 1981 on a sharing basis with British Airways. However, when British Airways Highland Division was set up in an attempt to reverse the state carrier's losses on internal Scottish routes they were given a two year period to prove themselves during which they were to be protected from direct competition from other airlines wanting to operate parallel services. Loganair could thus hope for no immediate expansion on the more dense Scottish internal routes yet routes of this kind are important in order to help offset the fragile viability of third level services. Loganair had to look southwards if it were to expand and application was made for British Airways' Edinburgh—Manchester service. For four months British Airways fought off Loganair's designs on the route, but then the service became one of seventeen routes axed by the state carrier as it strived to attain profitability. Loganair took over the Edinburgh—Manchester route in October 1982 only days after the announcement by British Airways of their plans to withdraw.

Manchester became a major new destination for Loganair. The link from Edinburgh was at first operated three times daily with the Shorts 330. During 1983 the Shorts 360 also appeared on the route and at the end of that year the forty-four-passenger Fokker Friendship was acquired for this service. On 11th January 1984 the Fokker Friendship was involved in an accident at Manchester after which it was withdrawn for repairs to the belly of the aircraft, a major overhaul and refurbishment. During that period the largest aircraft ever to fly for Loganair, in the form of a seventy-six-passenger Vickers Viscount, appeared on the Edinburgh—Manchester service. Despite the unfamiliar blue of British Air Ferries from whom it was leased, there was nonetheless no mistaking that the four engined prop-jet named 'The Flying Scotsman' was in the service of Loganair. The Shorts 330 and Shorts 360 went into another new service from Manchester to Belfast Harbour in 1983. Meanwhile the Fokker Friendship operated the first scheduled service to London Heathrow in Loganair colours, but from the Isle of Man on charter to Manx Airlines, in 1984.

That year ended with the Friendship operating on more familiar ground with, in addition to the Manchester to Edinburgh service, the start of a new scheduled service from Manchester to Glasgow, the introduction of which marked the successful conclusion of a five year plan during which the airline had set itself an objective of widening its operating base outwith Scottish internal services as the opportunity to open up major new internal routes had disappeared for the immediate future. Routes had been identified and the appropriate licences had been vigorously sought with a well-prepared battle plan. From 1980 to 1984 Loganair had aimed to launch a new trunk route annually and this they succeeded in doing with the routes Edinburgh—Belfast, Glasgow—Belfast, Edinburgh—Manchester, Belfast—Manchester and finally Glasgow—Manchester.

In 1985 and 1986 the emphasis has been on consolidating these routes and progressively upgrading the service. On the routes from Glasgow and Edinburgh to Belfast, Twin Otters and Shorts 330s have been replaced by Shorts 360 aircraft; and on the Manchester services the Shorts 330s which inaugurated them have been replaced by the Fokker Friendship and Shorts 360s. In addition to larger aircraft, greater frequencies of flights have increased passenger carryings; and the growing number of passengers has been enticed by the increasing sophistication of in-flight service — in-flight catering, free newspapers, hot towels and bar service.

Despite the glamour of these routes, the islands were yet to see a development in scheduled services, albeit a small one, in 1986 when a seasonal service was launched between Kirkwall and Fair Isle. The linking of the Loganair networks in Orkney and Shetland which this brought about is significant for islanders, general tourists and ornithologists alike in drawing the two island groups a little closer together.

It is the scheduled services of Loganair which are most in the public eye and they are likely to become more so as the years pass by. Aircraft change, colour schemes occasionally change, even the uniforms of the staff change. Originally the Loganair girls wore a blue tunic with a kilt in the Logan tartan where blue is also the predominant colour. By 1973 the uniform consisted of a red and white kilt or trousers and a duffle coat, ideal for windswept island airfields. This in turn was replaced by a very becoming uniform of red hat, black jacket and red skirt, as eye-catching as that worn by the personnel of any other airline. In 1984 the girls appeared in a new grey tartan uniform displaying the sophistication that you would expect of Scotland's airline. In 1986 the Twin Otter fleet started to appear with a new colour scheme. The familiar black belly was to disappear and be replaced with white and grey paintwork with lining in red and black. The Islander fleet is to receive similar treatment in 1987.

Captain Duncan McIntosh
Photo by Randak Design

previous page
Shorts 330
Glasgow, 1979
Photo by the author

Gil Fraser, Captain Duncan McIntosh, Captain Ken Foster and Scott Grier with one of the red DHC Twin Otters of the Royal Antarctic Survey
Photo by Randak Design

Charter

The charter activities of Loganair have been many and varied over the years. In the early days all outside work undertaken by the company was on a charter basis. Sometimes this involved a long term contract — for example, the flights to St Kilda literally to drop supplies to the Army, delivery of computer cards to Blackpool for the Post Office Savings Bank, carriage of football coupons to Belfast and Liverpool, and of course the famous newspaper run to Stornoway which operated for ten years without one morning's delivery being missed.

Unusual assignments included the provision of photographic target aircraft for gunners of the Territorial Army to practice on and the dropping of trainee parachutists of the Norwegian Army. Another contract saw a Loganair Aztec scattering dry ice crystals five hundred feet above fogbound Glasgow Airport during 1966 and 1967. The exercise was to disperse freezing fog and so keep the airport open to inbound aircraft. The crushed ice had the effect of lowering the temperature of the fog which precipitated as snow. Initial results were cause for cautious encouragement to the officials of Glasgow Corporation, owners of Glasgow Airport at that time, who had chartered the aircraft for these flights. After two winters the fog and the demand for the facility disappeared with the widespread introduction of smokeless zones in the area.

Much work was in the form of ad hoc charters, such as air taxi flights for businessmen, and in this respect no two days would be alike for the pilots. Ad hoc charters would also carry urgent goods such as succulent lobsters landed by Lewis fishermen which were flown from Stornoway to Continental markets. Loganair aircraft were also in much demand by photographers, both from the media and from survey companies.

Photographic work was undertaken for the film industry too. The first production involving Loganair was "633 Squadron". Much of the action was depicted as taking place in Norway, but in fact the dramatic shots of Mosquitos soaring up Norwegian fjords were filmed in Scotland. The local knowledge of the pilots was invaluable to the film producers as they could often suggest locations in Scotland that matched up with the geographical features required by the script and which would uphold the illusion that the filming had been undertaken in Norway. After "633 Squadron" Loganair tended to be involved in a production on an annual basis for several years and they assisted with the making of such films as "Goldfinger", "Ring of Bright Water", and "Zeppelin".

The charter of an aircraft comes into its own when time is a vital factor. During a General Election the results from island constituencies were often the last to be declared, often long after election fever had already subsided. Orkney and Shetland determined no longer to be in that position when an election was called in 1970 and Loganair was entrusted with the job of rushing the ballot boxes from both island groups to the count in Kirkwall.

Storm-bound islands have often been grateful for the appearance of the familiar red, black and white aircraft. Remote Foula has been one such beneficiary, while North Ronaldsay has been another. High seas had prevented the inter-island steamer from docking at North Ronaldsay for two weeks in the winter of 1969 and the island became short of provisions, most notably bread. A call was put out to the neighbouring island of Sanday where the baker immediately prepared an extra 180lb of bread and Loganair beat the weather to perform the necessary airlift. Four years later Loganair was participating in another airlift with Skyvan, Beech 18 and Islander aircraft carrying supplies of flour, sugar, butter and other provisions to Shetland which had been cut off for two weeks as the result of a dockers strike.

It seems that air and sea transport are frequently inter-related. In addition to coming to the rescue when shipping services are suspended as a result of weather conditions or industrial action, Loganair has also been called in when ships have been disabled by mechanical problems. Ship's spares have been flown to ailing vessels stranded in ports as far afield as Rotterdam, Hamburg and Bergen. When fishermen from the Orkney island of Shapinsay were going to collect a boat from Kristiansand in Norway in 1974 it therefore seemed appropriate to charter the Orkney-based Islander to take them there. Loganair was also on call when the Orkney Isles Shipping Company's vessel 'Islander' fouled her propeller at North Ronaldsay and a diver had to be flown out to her rescue.

When the RAF were installing new radar equipment at Saxa Vord, a massive Beverley C1 transport aircraft, capable of carrying twenty tons of cargo, was employed to carry the load to Sumburgh. Then it was Loganair's turn to move in under the wing of this aircraft, which reduced even the Skyvan to diminutive proportions, and provide the final link to Unst spread over five flights. When it came to unorthodox loads the Skyvan came into a role of its own — carrying items such as a beach buggy to an Autocross event at Inverness and a Landrover to the Isle of Coll. Its rear door had already proved its usefulness to the Norwegian Parachute Regiment so it was an appropriate aircraft for a stunt involving parachutists mounted on bicycles making a jump from eight thousand feet. Parachutists and bicycles parted company in mid-air to make separate descents at Barry near Dundee. The Skyvan also saw airborne the first part of the Lockheed Tristar jetliner when it carried the forging for the nose gear of the prototype, cast at Carron Ironworks in Falkirk, from Glasgow to Staverton in Gloucestershire.

For birds flight usually comes naturally. But Loganair has got in on the act on more than one occasion with feathery cargoes. Of course when several thousand day-old chicks travelled on the Beech 18 from Prestwick to Belfast it would have been a bit much to expect them to do it their way. The racing pigeons that were flown to the Faroes in the Skyvan were more used to travelling long distances under their own power. Unfortunately, after they were released a gale blew up, most of the five hundred and forty-three birds were scattered and only a few of the pigeons completed the homing flight.

In 1968 the Royal Society for the Protection of Birds undertook to re-establish the white-tailed eagle on Fair Isle and the first three of the species travelled on a special charter from Norway. A fourth white-tailed eagle followed on the scheduled service from Stavanger to Glasgow. Bird-watchers bound for the observatory on Fair Isle have also been frequent charterers of Loganair's aircraft.

But it is not only birds who fly, whether by their own efforts or by Loganair. Four-legged creatures are quite at home in the air, such as the nanny goat who flew by scheduled flight from North Ronaldsay to Sanday and left behind a small memento of her appreciation — on the floor. A less usual cargo was the three Shetland ponies which

Shetland ponies were re-introduced to Fair Isle after 80 years with the aid of a Loganair Islander
Photo by Dave Wheeler

A Shorts 360 is loaded up at Glasgow on a summer night in 1985 for one of the regular mail flights
Photo by the author

ROUTINE   007

R 271000Z   SIGNAL CENTRE
FM SUNRAY HIRTA (CAPT LEWIS)   28 MAR 1964
TO MOLAR MINOR (RQMS ROLPH)   SER No. 29007
                                             632 SIGNAL TROOP
UNCLAS G/101 PLEASE CONVEY FOLLOWING MESSAGE IN SIGNAL   (HEBRIDES)
TO THE PILOTS OF LOGANAIR.
ALL RANKS ST KILDA DETACHMENT THANK PILOTS OF
LOGANAIR FOR THEIR SPLENDID SERVICE DURING THE PAST TWELVE
MONTHS. DURING THE LONG WINTER WE WERE ALL VERY MUCH AWARE
THAT YOU WOULD GET OUT TO US WHENEVER THE WEATHER ALLOWED
AND GUNNERS HERE HAVE WATCHED WITH SATISFACTION THE
ARRIVAL ON TARGET OF ALL THAT YOU HAVE DROPPED TO US.
THANK YOU

ROUTINE

travelled in specially constructed boxes on an Islander from Sumburgh to Bergen in November 1972. Another ten Shetland ponies made the same journey to Bergen on board a Trislander one year later to go to a new home in Molde some two hundred miles further up the Norwegian coast. In March 1974 a further three of these sturdy little ponies flew from Sumburgh to Fair Isle bringing about a reintroduction of Shetland ponies to the island after an absence of eighty years. Racehorses and prize cattle were regularly freighted on the Skyvan. Amphibious creatures were not to be left out, four seals having comprised the cargo on a flight from Edinburgh. Their destination was the island of Texel off the north coast of the Netherlands.

One of the most unusual livestock consignments took place in 1986 and used a series of scheduled services. Hedgehogs introduced to the islands of North Ronaldsay and Papa Westray some years earlier had increased their numbers to such an extent that they were harassing island bird colonies having developed a taste for the eggs. Loganair was called in to redistribute the prickly population and hedgehogs were flown via Kirkwall to Edinburgh as part of the dispersal process.

The peak of Loganair's charter activities came during its involvement in oil support flights, an era which is now over. However, other charter commitments remain, most notably the air ambulance contract which has been held in full since 1973 and with a secondary role having been undertaken during the preceding six years; and contracts for the Post Office for night mail flights to Liverpool, East Midlands and Luton which have made a significant contribution to improving the company's financial position. Ad hoc charter work plays a very small role in the airline's activities in the eighties but if you want to hire your own aircraft Scotland's airline will be pleased to accommodate you whenever they are able.

Bullocks from the Isle of Man disembark from the Skyvan at Manchester en route to South America
Photo by courtesy of Captain Ken Foster

Oil Support

With the arrival of the seventies the oil bonanza in the North Sea was with us and the black gold-rush was on. Loganair's first involvement in oil support flying was in the form of a contract for Shell from December 1973. Loganair's first Trislander was based at Sumburgh and operated a service between Aberdeen and Sumburgh from which personnel continued by helicopter to the North Sea rigs.

After a year the number of personnel being flown on the service had increased to such a level that this contract was transferred to Dan-Air using the larger Hawker Siddeley 748. Loganair still had its sights set on the oil business and moved its oil support base to Aberdeen under the management of Captain Keith Alderson. Two Britten-Norman Trislanders were based in Aberdeen and these were kept busy on short term contracts, generally lasting from three to six months, for companies working on exploration wells.

Oil support flying was highly competitive with many operators arriving at Aberdeen intent on a piece of the action and with many going out of business in the process. Under-utilisation of aircraft was perhaps one of the biggest problems at this time as much of the flying involved ferrying personnel from Aberdeen to Sumburgh where they would continue out to the North Sea by helicopter. Sumburgh was not geared to handle this sudden volume of traffic and major congestion problems ensued to the extent that it was frequently late in the afternoon before the return passenger complement had arrived from offshore and was ready to continue south to Aberdeen; thus an aircraft might only get three to four hours flying in a day.

Loganair ordered its first DHC Twin Otter to undertake a contract for Occidental in 1977, a contract that was to fall through at the eleventh hour leaving Loganair with a new expensive aircraft with nowhere to go. Fortunately Loganair did not find it difficult to obtain other contracts for the Twin Otter and indeed found itself in a unique situation with this aircraft because of its excellent STOL capabilities. These qualities enabled the aircraft to operate into Unst, avoiding the congestion at Sumburgh, and oil companies wishing to operate their helicopter ferrying flights from there and bypass the frustration of Sumburgh, turned gratefully to Loganair and its Twin Otters.

Loganair served many oil companies, such as Conoco, Union Oil, Sun, Total, BNOC, Burmah Oil and Elf, but its biggest customer was Chevron Oil for whom a contract commenced in 1979, again flying to Unst. Six Twin Otters, and sometimes a seventh, representing thirty per cent of the Loganair fleet, were flying for Chevron out of Aberdeen and the operation at Dyce had grown to such an extent that a new three hundred thousand pound hangar and office block was built there in 1980. Latterly Chevron wished to switch to the larger DHC Dash 7, carrying fifty passengers and also with a STOL capability which would permit operation from Unst's 2,100 ft. runway. Loganair tendered for the new contract and an order was placed with De Havilland for the Dash 7. However the contract was awarded to Brymon Airways who had ordered three of these aircraft so Loganair's order was cancelled.

The two Brazilian built Embraer Bandeirantes joined the oil support fleet and with their longer range capability they flew to destinations such as Stavanger, Amsterdam and Cork on short-term contract work.

In 1979 a new terminal and helicopter runway were opened at Sumburgh but by this time a new generation of helicopters, such as the Puma and the Chinook, were operating on the North Sea. These helicopters were able to fly direct from Aberdeen to oil platforms in the East Shetlands basin obviating the need for fixed wing aircraft. By the early eighties Loganair was therefore gradually extracting itself from oil support flying in order to concentrate on the considerable and more stable scheduled network that had been built up over the previous decade. In 1983 a portion of the large hangar at Aberdeen was rented to British Airways Helicopters and October 1984 signalled the end of an era when the Aberdeen base was closed and the premises at Dyce Airport were put up for sale.

The oil companies were often demanding customers and there are undoubtedly mixed feelings surrounding the heady boom days now that they are past. Loganair's Twin Otter fleet attained a peak of nine aircraft and by 1980 forty per cent of its total fleet was dedicated to the oil industry. At that time only Dan-Air had more aircraft serving the oil industry from Aberdeen. However, dependence on the oil industry had its dangers and the period is probably best regarded as an era which stimulated the development of other activities which would endure when the oil support market could no longer be relied upon.

A patient arrives at Renfrew on a De Havilland Rapide of Scottish Airways in the nineteen-thirties

Scottish Airways also used the Spartan Cruiser for Air Ambulance duties
Photos by courtesy of Captain Eric Starling

The Scottish Air Ambulance Service

The initial decision on the need for an air ambulance flight rests not with large city hospitals, airline executives or government departments, but with the person most familiar with the needs of the patient — the local doctor. And in reaching his decision he will take into account not just the medical condition of his patient, but also the terrain and conditions, such as long or rough sea crossings and lurching jolts over unsympathetic roads, which his patient must endure in reaching hospital.

Having made the decision and arranged accommodation for his patient at the city hospital, the doctor calls the appropriate air ambulance base, just as his opposite number in the city would call a road ambulance. From the moment of his call a whole series of activities gets under way, carried out by very different people, but each an essential member of the air ambulance team.

Engineers make a final check of the aircraft, always kept in readiness twenty-four hours a day. The pilot is alerted and briefed on the flight with any special instructions, such as the most suitable altitude at which to fly, perhaps dictated by the patient's condition. The nurse is also alerted, her equipment kept at the ready, but perhaps supplemented by any additional items warranted by the patient's case. Within a short time pilot and nurse are taxying off and within a few hours the patient will have been collected from one of the Hebridean or Northern Isles or perhaps a remote part of the mainland and will be receiving the appropriate specialist treatment in one of the city hospitals.

The well-tried efficiency of the air ambulance service makes many an emergency into an uneventful routine procedure, despite the obvious anxieties harboured by any patient en route to hospital. The routine can, however, be upset by the elements as Mrs Morag Sinclair of Castlebay, Barra, recalls when she was due to go to Glasgow for an operation on 20th February 1971.

The prevailing winter gales had already postponed the ambulance flight by a day when she was taken to the beach airstrip at Northbay to join the expected aircraft. However, the weather was doing its worst and the aircraft was prevented from landing at Barra, having to divert to Benbecula. A solution to the problem was provided when someone suggested that the ferry for South Uist might still be moored at Eoligarry on the north tip of Barra.

Sure enough, the small open boat had not yet sailed and Mrs Sinclair's stretcher was laid amongst a party returning from a concert held on Barra the previous night, while her seventeen-year-old daughter kept her company. The ferry struggled through six miles of wild seas to Ludag, spray coming into the vessel leaving the deck awash and making the ailing patient quite wet by the time South Uist was reached.

An ambulance completed the road journey to Benbecula, with a stop at the Creagorry Hotel for hot water bottles. Mrs Sinclair recalls the welcome sight of air ambulance nurse Gisela Thürauf at Benbecula Airport as she was greeted with warm dry blankets and made comfortable on board the waiting aircraft.

Miss Thürauf recalls that particular night well. "We had been unable to land at Barra because of strong winds and the conditions were extremely turbulent with icy winds gusting as we flew north to Benbecula. Landing at Balivanich was difficult and once on the ground I could hardly stand upright without being blown over at the airport. The tail of the aircraft had to be stabilised and ballast put on board to prevent it toppling over.

"Mrs Sinclair was suffering from exposure and it was so cold on the ground that we had to wait until we had taken off and the aircraft had heated up before I could change her clothes and blankets. The Heron aircraft had pipes running along the inside of the cabin and I recall the aircraft taking on the appearance of a wash house as I made use of these to dry out Mrs Sinclair's clothing.

"Also on board the same flight was twelve-year-old James MacNeill from Vatersay whose hand had been crushed against Vatersay Pier by a boat. James had endured two ferry crossings, from Vatersay to Castlebay and from Eoligarry to Ludag, but being mobile he had escaped being soaked during these."

Mrs Sinclair reached Glasgow five hours after leaving Castlebay and once she was admitted to hospital only one problem remained. With a postal strike in progress and with gales disrupting the telephone network it was then difficult for her to contact her family at home to assure them of her well-being. But with the hospital sojourn completed, the trip home was more direct and less eventful.

BEA used De Havilland Rapides *above* **and later Herons** *below* **as air ambulances on flights such as these into Barra** *Both photos by courtesy of the RAF Museum, Hendon and British Airways*

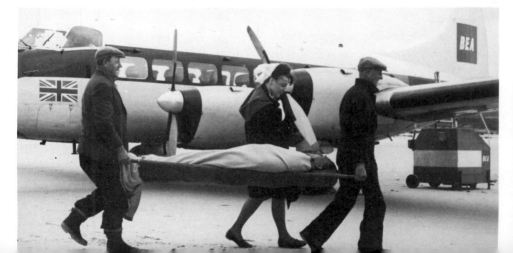

A Little History

The very first air ambulance flight took place on 14th May 1933. The patient was John McDermid, a thirty-three-year-old fisherman from Islay. He was suffering from perforation of the stomach and the threat of peritonitis was very real. Time was of the essence and his doctor sent a telegram to the St Andrew's Ambulance Association requesting the aid of an aircraft.

Midland and Scottish Air Ferries answered the call and soon one of their Dragon Moths (G-ACCZ) under the command of Captain J H Orrell was landing on the sands near Bridgend to collect Mr McDermid. Mrs A W Ferguson, a nurse from Glasgow who was holidaying on Islay at the time, accompanied the patient on the flight back to Renfrew. Mr McDermid was quickly transferred by ambulance to Glasgow's Western Infirmary where a successful operation was performed. The air ambulance service had arrived.

On 19th July 1933 Midland & Scottish Air Ferries undertook the first mercy flight to Skye. This time the patient was a Dr Fothergill who was on holiday on the island when he took ill at Uig. The air ambulance landed five miles north of Uig at Kilmuir and with the patient joined by his wife and a local doctor it proceeded to do its best to evade thunder, lightning and heavy rain with some skilful low altitude flying en route to Edinburgh Royal Infirmary.

Further north Captain Fresson of Highland Airways was soon pioneering air ambulance flights in the Orkneys where patients would be flown from the surrounding islands to the Orkney mainland or, when the need arose, from Orkney to mainland Scotland.

The first air ambulance flight from Shetland took place on 1st May 1937. Alex MacRae, the lighthouse keeper at Eshaness near Hamna Voe had taken seriously ill and his doctor did not rate highly his chances of surviving a long sea and road journey. Northern Lighthouses chartered a Dragon Moth from Allied Airways and, after a slight delay caused by fog, the pilot, Captain Vallance, was taxying the aircraft on a strip of grass cleared by Mr MacRae's son and daughter only fifty yards from the lighthouse. Mr MacRae was accompanied on the four hour flight to Edinburgh by his wife and the local district nurse, Mrs. McVie. On arrival he was transferred to the Royal Infirmary.

The early air ambulance flights were run very much on an ad hoc basis, but their life-saving qualities were quickly realised by those living in remote communities who could find themselves in a serious predicament whenever severe illness or injury arose. The value of the air ambulance was very apparent, but the cost of paying for such a flight was completely outwith the pocket of the vast majority of its potential users.

Local authorities did their bit to support the service, but local communities devised their own schemes to fund the service for their members. On Barra, concerts and ceilidhs were held to fund mercy flights for the island, while in Kintyre subscriptions were collected for an air ambulance insurance scheme. On Islay the laird of Kildalton Estate set up a trust fund into which the profits of activities such as sales of work, whist drives and concerts were paid.

Two events took place in 1947 which formalised the air ambulance service. One of these was the formation of the National Health Service which saw funding for the service being made the responsibility of the Department of Health for Scotland (now the Scottish Home and Health Department).

The other event of 1947 was the creation of British European Airways following the nationalisation of the various independent Scottish airlines. BEA used a De Havilland Rapide to operate the service, occasionally supplemented with a DC-3. In March 1955 a De Havilland Heron performed its first air ambulance flight and these hardy four-engined aircraft remained the backbone of the service until 1973 when Loganair took over full responsibility from the state airline, by that time operating as British Airways.

Before relinquishing the service to Loganair, British Airways performed one notable flight on 25th January 1973 when they flew Mrs Ann Heads from Islay to Glasgow to have a baby. It was perhaps appropriate that Mrs Heads should come from Islay for she was to be the ten thousandth patient to benefit from the Scottish Air Ambulance Service. When Mrs Heads returned home with her baby, Mr John McDermid, the fisherman carried on the first flight forty years before, was among those at Glenegedale Airport to meet her.

Life-saving Islanders

Loganair's first air ambulance flight took place on 16th June 1967 when Captain Ken Foster piloted Piper Aztec C G-ASYB on a flight from Oronsay to Glasgow.

However it was the arrival of the Britten-Norman Islander that really provided the introduction of air ambulance flights to Loganair's sphere of operations from 1967. At that time the service was operated by BEA, but while their De Havilland Herons were well-suited to provide air ambulance flights to the seven airfields then served, the short take-off and landing capabilities of the Islander provided Loganair with an opportunity to play a supplementary role to that of BEA by operating into some of the most basic airstrips which had previously been denied inclusion in the service.

Initially Loganair provided air ambulance services from Coll, Colonsay, Oronsay, Mull and Oban. Further airstrips were soon included in the service and following the retiral of BEA's Herons, Loganair was awarded the full air ambulance contract by the Scottish Home and Health Department from 1st April 1973.

Loganair carried almost ten thousand patients in the ten years following the award of the full air ambulance contract, approximately the same number as were carried in the preceding forty years. These figures do not suggest that the service is called out on any pretext, but they illustrate the massive development that has been possible during that time in bringing the service closer to an increasing number of communities, over fifty airstrips now providing access to the life-saving Islander air ambulances.

Widening the Net

It goes without saying that Loganair's pilots and the volunteer nurses have continued the tradition of the air ambulance service with the valour that has been its hallmark from the very earliest days, using a well-tried system to cheat the most atrocious flying conditions when life is at stake.

However, a keynote of the Loganair era has been the introduction of the service to new areas. In the nineteen-thirties the aircraft of the period under the command of skilled pioneering aviators would land on a dinner plate if it were flat enough and with sufficient space to permit take-off again. Those days have gone with even the most rugged modern aircraft demanding some conformity of procedures. But Loganair has been something of a pioneer too in introducing scheduled services to many small communities particularly in Orkney and Shetland, and even more points have been brought on line by them for air ambulance flights. In addition to places already mentioned, in the Hebrides there are Jura, Berneray, Northton (Harris) and Sollas (North Uist); in Orkney there are Egilsay, Hoy, Flotta, Shapinsay and Wyre; while in Shetland air ambulances serve Papa Stour, Foula and Out Skerries when a call goes out. These are the kind of islands that are envisaged in connection with the service, but of course it is available to all suitable airfields including those closer to "civilisation" when the circumstances are appropriate.

There are three bases operated by Loganair for air ambulance services. Air ambulances are maintained at both Kirkwall and Lerwick where their presence makes the service available in the shortest possible time to the many islands that form Orkney and Shetland. In addition to carrying patients to Kirkwall and Lerwick, the island-based air ambulances make frequent trips to Aberdeen, Glasgow and Edinburgh when the specialist treatment offered by one of the large city hospitals is required.

The principal air ambulance base is at Glasgow and this location receives most of its calls from the Inner and Outer Hebrides and from Kintyre. It is manned twenty-four hours a day, every day of the year, as are Kirkwall and Lerwick, and a call is never turned down. While weather can delay flights the effort is always made to reach the location of the patient, with assistance from a variety of quarters when necessary. On Mull for example the Coastguards have proved invaluable in providing local weather information to assist air ambulances make the journey to Glenforsa airstrip in the worst conditions.

Sometimes two or three days can pass without there being a call-out, but with an average of a thousand air ambulance missions each year it also happens that call-outs can occur simultaneously. An aircraft en route to transfer a patient home after treatment may in such a case be diverted in mid-flight to the location of a more pressing demand; even aircraft such as the Twin Otter have been press-ganged into ambulance duty upon occasion when the Islanders have already been out on call. On one August day five of Loganair's fleet were airborne on ambulance flights at the same time whilst a sixth aeroplane was prepared for yet another urgent call.

The greatest nightmare for island doctors is to be called to the scene of a car accident, house fire or similar calamity, which can produce several serious casualties requiring

Today Loganair's Britten-Norman Islanders provide air ambulance flights to an unprecedented number of airfields

Photos by courtesy of Captain Duncan McIntosh

A patient is tended by a nurse on board one of Loganair's life-saving Islanders

an airlift, knowing that the capacity of the Islander, and of many airstrips, is limited. Upon occasions such as these, the sense of isolation for a small island community can make itself very apparent, but fortunately major disasters do not occur too frequently.

Patients with broken backs or broken necks present special problems because of the difficulties in moving them. For such cases a special stretcher is used which suspends the patient from a frame maintaining a level position with minimal pressure no matter what angle is taken up by the aircraft during flight. The Glasgow air ambulance base handles all psychiatric patients, including any from Orkney and Shetland, for the nursing staff there have received specialist training in the handling of these cases. Two nurses will often accompany such flights, and occasionally a heavy policeman will also be in attendance.

Flying the seriously ill or injured to hospital in an emergency is a serious business — deadly serious. But even here there is often room for a smile (after the event at least) — as in the case when a doctor called an air ambulance for a small boy with "a foreign body in his foot". It turned out that it was the boy's foot that was in a foreign body when he was loaded on to the aircraft with his big toe firmly lodged in a bath tap — which had been persuaded to part company with the bath prior to the flight.

While the air ambulance service is mainly a domestic affair, flights are made to points further afield from time to time. With increasing frequency calls are received for a heart transplant patient to be flown to London and, in order to make the final road journey to Papworth Hospital as comfortable as possible for the patient, the Air Force have assisted by making RAF Wyton available to Loganair. Indeed the RAF have made airfields within Scotland available to air ambulance flights on many occasions too. In a few instances flights have been made to Norway when the passengers have usually been injured oil industry employees being repatriated by their company. It was a Norwegian seaman who benefited from the first Loganair international air ambulance flight when he was flown from Kirkwall to Bergen in June 1973. His leg had been crushed by a ship docking in Stromness harbour.

Loganair pilots have been outstanding in carrying on the tradition established by the early pioneers in flying in the worst conditions when life has been at stake. The debt owed by numerous beneficiaries of the mercy flights operated by these courageous aviators cannot be quantified.

Florence Nightingales of the Skies

A vital member of the crew on any air ambulance flight is the nurse, and very special people they are. The Glasgow-based air ambulance operation is staffed by nurses from the city's Southern General Hospital who are further trained in air ambulance duties. Yet it is not just another day's work for the team of nurses for their air ambulance duties are performed on a voluntary basis, often during their off-duty time.

The air ambulance nurse will arrive at the airport already briefed on the patient to be carried so that hospital care effectively commences as soon as the patient is on board the aircraft.

After performing ten air ambulance flights each nurse is awarded a Silver Wings brooch, the only decoration not awarded by a nursing college that may be worn on a nurse's uniform.

Although the nursing profession is often seen as a female vocation, both sexes participate as air ambulance nurses and mentally ill patients are usually escorted by male nurses.

Several of this devoted group of people, including one particular male senior nursing officer, have served on hundreds of mercy flights. Their reward, in addition to the satisfaction of bringing relief to the suffering, is an honorarium for each flight of one guinea, the sum fixed in the nineteen-thirties!

In 1969 the Shorts Skyvan operated Loganair's international scheduled service to Stavanger
Photo by Short Brothers & Harland Ltd by courtesy of Captain Ken Foster

Loganair International

It may be thought that Loganair's claim to fame as an International Airline relates solely to a sixteen month period during 1969 and 1970 now consigned to the aeronautical archives. That was the period during which Loganair operated its scheduled service from Glasgow and Aberdeen to Stavanger (the first international scheduled route to be operated from Aberdeen by any airline for thirty years).

The service sought to satisfy a demand from businessmen, tourists and ethnic traffic which unfortunately failed to materialise in sufficient volume to prevent Loganair losing twenty-four thousand pounds on the venture before withdrawing the service. Sadly, it was a case of being there too early rather than too late as the route now supports both Air UK and Scandinavian Airlines who use much larger equipment than the Beech 18 and Skyvan used by Loganair in the pre-oil boom days of operating the service.

With the arrival of oil exploration and extraction in the nineteen-seventies Loganair was to become a familiar sight at Norwegian airports, such as Stavanger and Bergen, flying charters on behalf of oil companies. Charter flights have taken Loganair aircraft to most parts of Europe and a Bandeirante operated one charter as far south as Tunis on behalf of the oil industry. But it has not just been oil companies and the North Sea oil era that have seen the carrier being called upon to operate outwith Scottish skies. From Loganair's earliest beginnings charters were regularly performed to European destinations. Executives of the Logan Construction Co Ltd were among those early visitors to the Continent in Loganair Aztecs flying to points as far apart as Gibraltar and Finland.

Loganair has also operated aircraft outside the U.K. upon occasions and one of the earliest lasted from June until September 1969 when the Skyvan was based at Gardermoen in Norway. Its role there was to fly on behalf of the Norwegian Parachute Regiment for their parachutists to undertake training jumps, a role to which the Skyvan with its large rear cargo door was ideally suited.

Further afield Loganair had Trislander G-BDOM operating in Sudan from April until June 1982 while development of possible oil sources was being evaluated by the Sudanese Government. In the same year discussions took place which would have seen a Twin Otter operating in Libya but these did not come to fruition.

In a slightly different role, Loganair was in the Falkland Islands quite some time before the confrontation between the UK and Argentina brought this remote group of South Atlantic islands to the public attention in 1982. This was for the months of September, October and November 1979 when Captain Andy Alsop was seconded to the Falkland Islands Government Air Service to assist with the introduction of a land-based Britten-Norman Islander. Their fleet had previously comprised two Beaver floatplanes. Basic strips of grass or gravel were prepared and in some instances beaches were used for the new operation serving a population of a mere eighteen hundred souls scattered in settlements and on islands across an area equivalent in size to Wales. Landing hazards that might be encountered included flocks of penguins and the daunting mass of a four ton elephant seal.

The Falklands connection did not rest there. Twin Otters registered in Port Stanley and serving with the British Antarctic Survey teams came to Scotland upon several occasions to fly for Loganair in their distinctive red liveries during the winter months of the Southern Hemisphere. Twin Otter G-BEJP appeared in another colour scheme in 1982 when it set off to Angola on charter to the International Red Cross and was used for famine relief. The aircraft was all white except for the distinctive 'red cross' and for diplomatic reasons it was operated by Schreiner Airways of Holland in its role of ferrying food and medical supplies from Luanda to remote areas of Angola. For six months in 1986 Twin Otter SE-GEF was flying Loganair services in the blue and white livery of Swedair from whom it was leased.

Loganair aircraft which have passed to subsequent owners are now flying in many parts of the world. Indeed, so are many former Loganair pilots who have 'moved on', Sierra Leone seemingly having a special popularity. At one time it appeared that Sierra Leone Airways, with a domestic operation based on Trislander aircraft, relied completely upon former Loganair captains.

While Loganair aircraft have been sold off to far off lands to which it falls upon the new owners to transport them, the airline has also bought aircraft from abroad, particularly the aircraft of the Twin Otter fleet.

Here Loganair chooses to be responsible for ferrying the new aircraft to Glasgow and these delivery flights have provided a dramatic change from the short hops to which the fleet are more accustomed. Most of the Twin Otters were collected from De Havilland Canada at Toronto and a typical delivery route would take the aircraft to Sept-Iles in Quebec and Goose Bay in Newfoundland before setting out across the Atlantic. Fitted with ten forty-five-gallon overload tanks the aircraft would make a gradual ascent reaching an altitude of eighteen thousand feet once the excessive fuel load had been lightened, to be followed by a cruise descent. A stop would usually be made at Narssarssuak in Greenland although Captain Ken Foster recalls one delivery where this stop was omitted and touch down was made at the next port of call, Keflavik in Iceland, and still with sufficient fuel to take them on to Glasgow.

The longest Twin Otter delivery was that of G-BHFD undertaken by Captains Alan Whitfield and Ken Dempster both of whom had experience in Canadian skies. This aircraft was collected from Fields Aviation at Calgary and firstly flew to Churchill on the shores of Hudson Bay. It was December and the next port of call was to have been Frobisher Bay on Baffin Island, but because of a snow blizzard there an intermediate stop at Coral Harbour, on Southampton Island at the entrance to Hudson Bay, was added. From Frobisher Bay 'Foxtrot Delta' continued to Sondre Stromfjord in Greenland, thence to Keflavik and on from there to reach Glasgow after a total time in flight of eighteen hours.

The furthest journey made during any delivery flight was that made by Captain Jamie Bayley in delivering Embraer Bandeirante G-BIBE from the manufacturers in Brazil. This aircraft flew from São José dos Campos (just south of São Paulo) via Recife to the island of Fernando de Noronha. The flight proceeded across the Atlantic to Senegal then continued north by way of the Canary Islands and Wales. Revealing some of the adventure experienced on the Bandeirante delivery flight, Captain Bayley recalls the flight home:

DHC Twin Otter G-BHFD at Coral Harbour, Hudson Bay, Canada, during its delivery flight
Photo by Captain Alan Whitfield

Loganair rubbing shoulders with some of the world's great airlines at Amsterdam's Schiphol Airport
Photo by the author

"On 28th October 1980. myself and John White (Flight Administration Officer and Navigator) left São José dos Campos for Recife for customs clearance and formalities before proceeding to Fernando de Noronha, a small island in the South Atlantic which is part of Brazil and some three hundred and fifty nautical miles to the north east of Recife. From Fernando de Noronha our route was to Dakar in West Africa, Las Palmas, Cardiff, Glasgow.

"The aircraft carried a one thousand litre ferry tank and a portable Omega navigation system and portable HF set in addition to the normal avionics fit. The HF set did not ever function satisfactorily, but the Omega set was of great assistance and performed well throughout the trip.

"From São José to Recife took seven hours flight time in excellent weather.

"The business of clearing customs at Recife was both protracted and frustrating. Despite the fact that the aircraft was manufactured in Brazil and all the documentation was in order, it took some three hours to clear Recife. I had been hoping not to arrive at Fernando de Noronha during the hours of darkness as the only facility there is a NDB approach and scrutiny of the approach charts showed some very interesting spot heights in close proximity to the airfield.

"In the event we arrived in darkness.

"On establishing contact with the air traffic controller it was a surprise to discover he did not speak English (English being the international language employed in aviation).

"The night was spent in a Nissen Hut belonging to the Brazilian Army. It was in a state of disrepair and the toilet facilities are best left to the imagination.

"We visited the meteorological office which was a small hut on the airfield boundary at 0700 on the morning of the 29th. The meteorological officer (?) cleared a roosting chicken from his desk and produced our route forecast — a transcript of yesterday's weather at Dakar. Communications between Recife and Fernando had now broken down 'but may be working later, Signore'.

"So, armed with the previous day's newspaper, which included a satellite photograph of the South Atlantic weather pattern (it looked fine), we set off and duly arrived five minutes early at Dakar after an elapsed flight time of seven hours thirty minutes.

"The remainder of the flight was mainly mundane and hardly worthy of expansion.

"The routing was through Las Palmas — Cardiff — Glasgow arriving on the evening of the 30th October."

Loganair's activities at home have often been of interest to airlines and government bodies across the world and delegations have arrived on numerous occasions to evaluate the reasons for the success of operations such as that in Orkney in order that they may be adapted in similar island groupings in other countries.

Such visitors have come from places as far apart as New Zealand, Malaysia and the Falkland Islands. The Portuguese were keen to emulate the service in the Azores as were the Spaniards in the Balearic and Canary Islands while the Japanese were also keen to apply the Loganair formula to their offshore islands.

It is probably fair to say that Loganair is not quite the 'local' airline that one may be inclined to imagine and while it is many years since it played the role of international scheduled carrier, there is no reason to doubt that it may again and probably on a very different scale.

Keeping the Big Birds Flying

Certain sections of an airline's workforce are very much in the public eye, for example the airport check-in staff and the flight attendants, and often in the case of Loganair, especially on inter-island services operated by the Islander aircraft, the pilots. Taken for granted because everything works so smoothly are other staff such as those in operations, reservations and many administrative functions.

Ensuring that the aircraft are also there when they should be is a dedicated team of engineers lead by Gil Fraser. Gil Fraser is from Dingwall where he was responsible for maintaining the vehicle fleet of the Logan Construction Co Ltd. When Loganair was set up he recalls being asked by Willie Logan if he 'would pop down to Glasgow for six months to look after his plane', and he is still looking after the fleet of aircraft bearing the founder's name after more than two decades. Another long-serving member of the team was George Cormack, the Chief Engineer until 1984. When a schoolboy in the sixties, as an aviation enthusiast, he used to wash the Loganair aircraft at the weekends.

Loganair's engineering base is its hangar at Glasgow Airport where a team of sixty-eight engineers keep the fleet maintained to the very high standards demanded by the airline and of course by the Civil Aviation Authority in their criteria for the granting of an Air Operator's Certificate. There are also engineers at every base: Edinburgh — nine, Belfast — five, Kirkwall — three, Stornoway — two, and one at each of Lerwick and Manchester. An additional engineering unit was maintained at Kirkwall from 1976 until 1979 to maintain the Britten-Norman fleet, the Islanders and Trislanders, and this base serviced aircraft from Glasgow, Shetland and Stornoway in addition to the Orkney-based aircraft. Once the Trislanders had been replaced by the Twin Otters, servicing of the remaining Islanders was transferred to Glasgow.

The Loganair hangar is divided into two sections referred to as 'behind the curtain' and 'in front of the curtain'. The curtain retains one-third of the hangar as a heated area and handles a maintenance cycle from 8.00am to 5.00pm seven days a week. The area in front of the curtain is for operational maintenance and this is manned by three shifts twenty-four hours a day. The hangar also contains spares currently valued in excess of one-and-a-half million pounds — a lot of capital to have sitting on the shelf, but certainly less expensive than having surplus aircraft on permanent standby to take the place of a disabled machine grounded while the appropriate component is obtained. The high inventory of spares has been dictated by the multiplicity of aircraft types required by Loganair to carry out its extremely diverse range of activities.

Much of the work required on aircraft is undertaken as progressive maintenance — a systematic check of various items being carried out as part of a cycle whenever the aircraft is on the ground for a short time. However each aircraft is taken out of service at regular intervals. For the Islander this is every two hundred and fifty flying hours, when the aircraft is given a thorough going over lasting five days. For the DHC Twin Otter and the Shorts 360 a full maintenance programme is undertaken every one hundred and four hundred flying hours respectively. The Fokker Friendship is given line maintenance by Dan-Air with full maintenance being undertaken by BMA at East Midlands at the end of four months or five hundred flying hours, whichever comes first.

The engineering team ensure that a Britten-Norman Trislander is kept in top condition

Tiree's modest airport terminal extends a welcome to arriving passengers
Loganair's Twin Otter is prepared for departure from Tiree *Photos by the author*

While Loganair does not handle the maintenance of the Friendship it does undertake work for other operators such as Manx Airlines and Malinair.

The aircraft themselves establish their own reputations with the engineers, who have to be certified in respect of each aircraft type for CAA approval to carry out full maintenance on that type. Different types establish differing reputations. However, the Shorts 360 is held in particularly high regard. With scheduled service duties during the day and Post Office contract work well into the night, the Shorts 360 puts in some twenty hours of work each day of which a substantial nine hours are spent airborne.

With new aircraft the manufacturers provide courses for engineers in carrying out maintenance on that model. These courses are generally of three weeks' duration, so prior to the delivery of the first Embraer Bandeirante some key engineering staff enjoyed a three-week training course in Brazil. The engineers are used to thinking beyond the confines of the curtained hangar at Glasgow and if a Twin Otter requires a replacement part which is not in stock De Havilland Canada is only a phone call away. And, so good is De Havilland's customer support system, the item in question has usually reached Glasgow from Toronto by the following morning.

The engineers are used to working in the field too. Gil Fraser recalls many instances when engineers have had to work throughout the night to rectify defects and even change engines. In the days of the Stavanger service there was an occasion when a team had to fly to Norway in the Skyvan with a replacement engine for the Beech 18 which had become disabled there. The engineers spent three days in Stavanger restoring the Beech 18 to flying condition. Such instances are not restricted to historical times; recently engineers had to fly to East Midlands on a Saturday to undertake three days' repairs to a Shorts 360.

Islanders have had their share of bumps because of the rugged terrain and basic strips which are so often their normal territory. One Islander aircraft ended up in a stream on the island of Rousay in the Orkneys in February 1980 when landing in a gale. The airstrip on Rousay had just been opened and it had been the intention to use it for ambulance flights. However, it was declared unsuitable after that incident. The disabled aircraft, weighing two tons, had to be lifted by a Sikorsky S61 helicopter of Bristow Aviation to be flown the twelve miles to Kirkwall suspended below it; not an everyday occurrence fortunately, but the engineers take it all in their stride.

Tiree

Serving an Island Community

Loganair at present serves eighteen islands, scattered around Scotland's western and northern seaboards, with scheduled flights. Further islands have regular charter services and in addition to these there are still more islands to which an occasional charter will operate and which can also call upon the air ambulance service.

Archie MacArthur has been Station Manager on Tiree for over twenty years, formerly with BEA and latterly with Loganair which has provided the scheduled service from Glasgow since 1975.

Tiree is typical of the islands which depend on the services provided by Loganair as, apart from a ferry service which calls at the island three to four times per week, the air link is the only artery to the outside world.

Air services to Tiree originated in 1934 when Midland and Scottish Air Ferries Ltd used an airstrip by the shore at Tràigh Bhagh. With the coming of the Second World War this airfield was requisitioned by the RAF and tarmac runways were laid on The Reef for Coastal Command operations from 1942 until 1945. During this period, one of unprecedented activity on Tiree, aircraft operated as far north as Iceland gathering long-range weather forecast data. After the war BEA served the island by Rapides, and later by Herons, although there was a short period when a Dakota linked Tiree not only with Glasgow but also with Benbecula, Stornoway and Inverness. Shorts Skyliners made a brief appearance before Loganair took over the role of providing air services for the island. Reef Aerodrome, constructed for wartime use, continues to serve the Isle of Tiree today.

Tiree has a population of eight hundred and because of the tied crofting system on the island it is a highly indigenous community, whereas on other islands, such as neighbouring Coll, the native population is outnumbered by incoming settlers. A small knitwear factory operates on Tiree, but as it is one of the most fertile Hebridean islands crofting is the mainstay of the community.

The air service to Glasgow is therefore primarily a personal one in terms of the needs of the islanders, being used for trips to the mainland to visit relatives, to keep a hospital appointment, or by students travelling to college. From the mainland the route is used by officials, such as surveyors and engineers of Strathclyde Regional Council. Upon occasions the ferry schedule between Arinagour and Scarinish dovetails with the air service timetable enabling residents of Coll, which has a population of one hundred and thirty, also to use the Tiree—Glasgow flights. In the winter the aircraft continues from Tiree to Barra as it is expedient to operate a combined service to both islands at that time of year. There is little inter-communication between these two islands, but occasionally a commercial traveller, for example, will join the Barra-bound aircraft at Tiree. On the island where the community is close-knit passengers on the air service are often already well acquainted with each other.

Loganair's Glasgow—Tiree route is not just a passenger service. Some twelve kilos of first class mail arrives on each flight and as Christmas approaches this can increase to sixty kilos. Efficient operation of the mail service can be particularly important. For example, if a hospital appointment notification fails to arrive on time, a whole series of arrangements for a patient's treatment in hospital, including his air journey to Glasgow to attend, have to be re-arranged.

Additionally residents of Tiree rely on Loganair for their newspapers. Since the aircraft has to carry fuel for perhaps continuing to Barra and then returning to Glasgow, weight limitations are occasionally a problem. It is very rarely that the papers have to be left behind, but on these occasions Archie jokes that he finds it prudent to avoid a visit to either of the two shops at which they should have been on sale. Monday's flight carries a particularly heavy load of newspapers since the morning's papers are also accompanied by the Sunday editions.

The flight is also a boon to crofters who may need a replacement part for a car or tractor urgently. Such a need inevitably occurs in the midst of the harvest season when disabled machinery is a major inconvenience. However a phone call at 8.30am will often see the required component delivered at Reef Aerodrome by the scheduled flight only three hours later.

An inconspicuous plastic container, marked 'Batchelors Macaroni Noodles' makes a weekly visit to Glasgow on Loganair's Twin Otter. The receptacle contains a water sample from the island's water supply being sent for routine testing. Further containers are regularly brought from Mull and Coll on the ferry for onward despatch for similar testing. This is one example of the less obvious roles undertaken by the service.

The air ambulance service is of course only summoned in emergencies, but it is with that service also in mind that Archie MacArthur, himself a native of Tiree, comments that there is genuine gratitude throughout Tiree for the service provided by Loganair. Carrying over five thousand passengers annually, or six times the population of the island, there is no doubting the truth of that. And it is a sentiment which is echoed by the people of many more of the islands that form an arc around Scotland from Islay to Unst.

The Shorts 360 now operates many of Loganair's more dense routes   *Photo by the author*

Up and Away with BMA

When Loganair joined the British Midland group on 2nd December 1983 it became part of a family with a fine aviation pedigree. British Midland Airways had been operating under that name since 1st October 1964, but its first scheduled services commenced in 1953 when it flew from Derby to Jersey via Wolverhampton as Derby Airways. Derby Airways started charter operations six years earlier, in 1947, but the company's origins go back even further, to the establishment of Air Schools Ltd in October 1938.

When Loganair became a subsidiary of British Midland, the parent company already had forty-five years aviation experience behind it. Most recently, British Midland had broken a twenty-year monopoly when it won a licence to compete with British Airways on the Glasgow—London Heathrow route, offering traditional high standards of in-flight service as an alternative to the state airline's no-frills Shuttle service, and this service commenced in October 1982. Similar services commenced on the Edinburgh—London Heathrow route at the beginning of 1983. Simultaneously British Midland was trying to break another monopoly — that of Prestwick on trans-Atlantic flights — with an application to fly to New York from Glasgow Airport. While BMA had become an important part of the Scottish aviation scene in the nineteen-eighties, it was by no means a newcomer to Scotland having been operating to Glasgow from East Midlands, and from Derby before that, providing a service between the Midlands of England and Scotland which had operated for three decades.

In 1982 British Midland, with Air UK, had formed Manx Airlines, a new airline based on the Isle of Man to serve that island's transportation requirements. Manx Airlines operated with a great deal of autonomy while enjoying the support of a major airline as its parent company. A similar situation was to be applied to Loganair enabling it to continue to identify with the special needs of its passengers whether they be users of the growing network of commuter routes or those reliant on the carrier as lifeline to the islands. Chairman of British Midland Airways and Manx Airlines, Michael Bishop, became Chairman of Loganair Ltd. The day to day running of the airline, however, is in the hands of its Managing Director, Scott Grier, who now has a twenty-five per cent shareholding in Loganair.

A decision had been taken in June 1983 to acquire a forty-four-passenger aircraft and the twin turbo-prop Fokker Friendship (G-IOMA) had joined the fleet the month before the takeover. As it happened, the Friendship was leased from British Midland. This aircraft was based at Manchester and went into service on the Manchester—Edinburgh route.

In March 1984 the second Shorts 360 arrived, replacing the remaining Shorts 330. The Shorts 360s were now operating on services from Edinburgh to Belfast, Wick and Kirkwall, Glasgow to Belfast and Manchester to Belfast.

After a first year of consolidation, which saw the closure of the Aberdeen base following the withdrawal from oil support flights and the denial of a licence to operate a scheduled service from Aberdeen to Lerwick, Loganair had attained a break-even situation. Now poised to produce a profit in its second year as a member of the British Midland group, Loganair launched a new service with the Fokker Friendship, linking Glasgow with Manchester from October 1984.

By 1986 the emphasis was very much on scheduled service operations. The scheduled network now accounted for eighty-five per cent of Loganair's activities. The remainder, which represented charter work, consisted primarily of contract work for the Post Office and the operation of the Air Ambulance Service, while an aircraft based at Lerwick performed oil pollution surveillance flights from Scatsta for the Shetland Isles Islands Council Ports and Harbours. The Post Office mail contracts involved several aircraft operating night rotations with one Twin Otter operating Aberdeen—Glasgow—Liverpool—Glasgow while another operated Edinburgh—Liverpool—Edinburgh. Post Office flights Glasgow—East Midlands—Glasgow, Glasgow—Luton—Glasgow, Belfast—Luton—Belfast and Edinburgh—Luton—Edinburgh were operated by the Shorts 360s.

A major tragedy was, however, to befall Loganair in 1986 when Twin Otter G-BGPC crashed on 12th June during its approach to Glenegedale Airport, Islay, while on a scheduled flight from Glasgow. The fuselage remained intact and this had much to do with the fourteen passengers escaping with only minor injuries and shock, but the nose of the aircraft took the full impact killing Captain Christopher Brookes while co-pilot Captain David Ilsley sustained severe injuries. It was the airline's first serious accident and at a time of great stress for it some consolation at least could be taken from the support offered by the public and the praise given to the airline for its outstanding safety record while operating over some of the most rugged terrain.

While it is interesting to look back over the last twenty-five years, Loganair is constantly looking to the future and there are no doubt exciting chapters of Loganair's story yet to unfold in the years ahead.

Karen Castle-Mason, Miss Loganair 1985, shows off the interior spaciousness of the Shorts 360 — and the current uniform   *Photo by Flightpath/Print Centres Ltd, Isle of Man*

Photos by the author

The DHC Twin Otter,
seen here taking off
from Barra, serves on
many island routes

The Fokker Friendship
features on services
between Scotland and
Manchester

A Vickers Viscount
leased from British Air
Ferries in 1983/84 is
the largest aircraft to
have been operated by
Loganair

New aircraft are frequently evaluated and by 1985 inspections had been made of the Saab Fairchild 340, Dornier 228, and the French/Italian-built ATR 42. The Dornier 228 carries nineteen passengers and cruises at two hundred and thirty knots. With financial backing available to airlines developing new regional services to Europe under the British Airways largesse scheme, Loganair was interested in the Dornier 228 to operate potential European routes and as a Twin Otter replacement. The Dornier 228 was seen to be ideal for existing Twin Otter routes and would, for example, reduce the Edinburgh—Lerwick flight time from two hours to one hour and twenty-five minutes, but with an unpressurised cabin was not considered appropriate for proposed services to Brussels, Cologne, Copenhagen and Rotterdam. (This incidentally is not Loganair's first contact with the German aircraft manufacturer — the Dornier Do 28 was evaluated during the nineteen-sixties when preparations were being undertaken for the commencement of the Orkney internal services.) The Jetstream 31 was considered for the European routes, but without STOL capability it was unsuited to many island routes. So the launch of international services has been left for another time and instead immediate attention has been diverted to building upon existing services, especially the higher density routes between Glasgow, Edinburgh, Belfast and Manchester.

Capacity has been steadily increased on these routes by the operation of additional schedules and larger aircraft types. Larger numbers of passengers are being attracted by many innovations to the in-flight service which the larger aircraft facilitate. In August 1986 a measure of the carrier's success was witnessed when Loganair carried for the first time more than twenty-five thousand passengers in a month.

Other aircraft for the future include the British Aerospace Advanced Turbo-Prop (ATP) and the de Havilland Canada Dash 7. British Midland is the launch customer for the sixty-four-passenger ATP with the first due for delivery during 1987. It could eventually be a Loganair candidate for such routes as Edinburgh—Manchester. The DHC Dash 7 nearly joined Loganair's fleet in 1980, but it could yet join in 1987 in preparation for the launch of another airline planned within the British Midland group, Eurocity Express. Eurocity Express is BMA's bid to operate services from the London Stolport being built on disused docks in east London and the DHC Dash 7 is central to all airlines interested in the project. Proving flights using Belfast Harbour Airport in the months ahead would have certain merits.

But what of Loganair's role now on those basic airstrips which do not even lay claim to a scheduled service? As the airline looks to 'bigger things', the pioneering tradition in the backwoods of Scottish aviation is not being overlooked. This is particularly evident in the provision of the air ambulance service, for which over one thousand flights are now operated annually. An on-going project of developing new landing sites which would be available for this vital service saw new strips coming on line during 1985 on the Orcadian islands of Egilsay, Shapinsay and Wyre. And in the sphere of third level routes 1986 saw the launch of a new scheduled service linking Kirkwall with Fair Isle.

Another innovation on traditional island routes came in 1985 with the introduction of welcome and disembarkation messages in Gaelic as well as English on routes to the islands of the Hebridean group. The airline responded warmly to the suggestion of bilingualism which had come from Comunn na Gàidhlig and proceeded to develop the linguistic talents of ten cabin staff. Gaelic now also appears on the airline's boarding cards.

Some Personalities

The Nurse — Gisela Thürauf

The Scottish Air Ambulance Service has benefited on over seven hundred occasions from the enthusiasm and devotion of a singular woman. It was on 17th July 1965 that Gisela Elisabeth Thürauf, from her base at the Southern General Hospital in Glasgow, flew her first air ambulance mission, a flight to Islay.

Miss Thürauf's story does not however begin at that point, but reaches back through the mists of time and a distinguished ancestry which can be traced back to 1122. Gisela Thürauf was born in Wurtzburg, in the Lower Franconia region of Bavaria; it was in this area including parts of what are now modern Austria, Hungary and Czechoslovakia that various forebears of hers made their marks in such areas as the arts, medicine and high administrative office. In the sixteenth century one ancestor published the first German book on medicine for the common man, while another published a volume on art covering every facet down to the decorative metalwork used on swords and daggers. Another member of the family attained a high rank in the service of the Holy Roman Emperor, Charles V. In more recent times Miss Thürauf's grandfather made important research into grains and soils on the Baltic and his work is commemorated in the names given to some of these grains.

The Nazi era, however, changed the family's fortunes. They were not in good favour with Hitler's regime, their properties were confiscated and it was as a refugee that Gisela Thürauf arrived in the United Kingdom after the Second World War.

Miss Thürauf is now a full-time nursing officer at the Southern General Hospital. Her air ambulance duties have, however, always been performed on a voluntary basis in her off-duty hours and Miss Thürauf can look back over a one hundred per cent success record since flying her first mission with BEA. Through skilful organisation and a special awareness of each individual's needs, she has always delivered her patients safely to the receiving hospital, no mean feat when it is recalled that many have been suffering from serious illness or severe multiple injuries when the air ambulance has been summoned to their aid.

Miss Thürauf recalls many specific incidents, such as an occasion when a patient had to be flown from Wick in severe snow blizzards which necessitated a six hour wait at Wick in the shelter of a hangar while snow was being cleared at the destination airport, Glasgow. She was nurse on an emergency flight to make a unique night landing performed on the beach at Barra, made in mid-winter with the aid of car lights, to come to the aid of a motor accident victim.

On another occasion it was not possible to land at Barra to uplift a small boy who had injured himself with the harbourmaster's gun. Miss Thürauf's organisational flair was instrumental in instigating arrangements for the boy to be taken by lifeboat to South Uist and then by ambulance to Benbecula where the air ambulance was able to land and take him for emergency treatment.

In acknowledgment of her first 500 air ambulance flights Gisela Thürauf was presented with a pair of special gold wings
Photo by The Glasgow Herald

Psychiatric patients have sometimes caused their own problems, such as the man who was quite insistent that he should leave the aircraft in mid-flight in order to attend mass. Miss Thürauf had to use her greatest powers of persuasion to convince him that it was too early for mass, and anyway the altar boys hadn't arrived yet.

Another unpleasant incident involved an extremely ill patient. Miss Thürauf was already concerned at his deteriorating condition when the patient emitted a massive volume of fluid and blood which hit the ceiling of the aircraft and rebounded over her. Such was her appearance as a result of this mishap that on arrival at the hospital with the patient, and with the identifying features of her uniform no longer apparent as a result of the incident, the receiving staff at first assumed that she was the one being admitted.

Flying has had its lighter moments too. On one occasion, not obviously on a mercy mission, and with a pilot who shall remain nameless, it was a tempting piece of mischief to flash out a morse message while flying low in the darkness. The message read "We want to make contact" and lines were soon buzzing with reports of a UFO sighting.

All air ambulance nurses receive their wings after their tenth flight, but in 1976 Loganair made a special award of a pair of gold wings to commemorate the achievement of five hundred flights by Miss Thürauf. The presentation was carried out by veteran air ambulance pilot Captain David Barclay. Gisela Elisabeth Thürauf, SRN, SCM, has now flown over eight hundred missions and attended over one thousand air ambulance patients. Her one thousandth patient was Mr Kenneth MacIntyre who flew from Benbecula to Glasgow on 12th July 1986.

In recognition of all these qualities Miss Thürauf was awarded the Queen's Commendation for "Valuable Service in the Air" — the only woman to have received the award in this category.

Additionally, throughout Scotland there are many who give Miss Thürauf their own special thanks for turning out at their special time of need, with one of the team of courageous pilots, in weather conditions so atrocious that most of us would be deterred from even venturing to the corner shop.

For relaxation Miss Thürauf enjoys the works of the great classical composers. Also she is a long standing associate member of the Iona Community through which she gains much inspiration for many of her activities, private and professional.

The Pilot — Captain Alan Whitfield

Newcastle born Alan Whitfield was bound for a career in farming when he set off for a new life in Canada. But after a time he left the land and studied at the Alberta College of Technology. He then joined the Texas Gulf Corporation and it was with them that he took to flying, the activity subsequently developing to the extent that he became a commercial pilot.

In 1962 Captain Whitfield returned to the UK and joined Carlisle-based Cumberland Aviation. Later he moved to Strathallan Air Services, but it was while serving with Cumberland Aviation that Captain Whitfield was loaned to the Scottish Flying Club as an instructor and this led to his introduction to Captain McIntosh.

It was not, however, until June 1969 that Alan Whitfield joined Loganair, the only pilot of that era to come without a background of RAF or Royal Navy flying. That was not to be a handicap and he was immediately sent to Shetland where his first role was that of pioneer and inspirer. In 1969 the Shetland Isles were served by Sumburgh Airport, with the only other airstrips being the newly constructed airstrip on Unst and the disused World War Two aerodrome at Scatsta. Alan set about convincing the Shetland Islanders that a network of airstrips could bring numerous benefits.

Captain Whitfield made his first landing on the remote island of Foula on 16th October 1969. The people of Foula immediately realised the advantages of having access to air services and the first make-shift airstrip was completed within three weeks, one small tractor being the only mechanical support available to supplement the picks and shovels of the islanders. The first passenger landed on Foula on 4th November and the first commercial flight took place with Loganair's Shetland-based Islander G-AVRA on 12th November 1969.

The value of Foula's airstrip was brought fully home in July 1970 when Leslie Bordman, a youth visiting the island on an adventure holiday, accidentally put his arm through a window causing severe blood loss. Such was the swiftness of Captain Whitfield's air ambulance operation that the injured boy was uplifted and back at Sumburgh before the ambulance to take him to hospital in Lerwick, summoned at the same time as the aircraft, had arrived at the Sumburgh terminal.

Captain Alan Whitfield is presented with the Queen's Commendation for 'valuable service in the air' by the Lord Lieutenant of Lanarkshire, Colonel The Rt Hon Lord Clydesmuir

Photo by Loganair News/Randak Design

The disadvantages of Sumburgh's location in the context of a local network of air services were readily apparent; and with much effort steps were successfully taken to establish an airfield adjacent to Lerwick. The first Tingwall airfield was on Church of Scotland property and its first flight was an ambulance flight to Fetlar, taking eighty-five-year-old Mrs Catherine Anderson home after a three month sojourn in Lerwick's Gilbert Bain Hospital. This flight also saw the first visit of an aircraft to Fetlar since a visit in 1939 by a De Havilland Rapide of Highland Airways.

Another herculean effort was successfully encouraged on Papa Stour where the runway was prepared entirely by the hard labour of the islanders equipped only with picks and shovels.

On Out Skerries the cost of ten thousand pounds required to build an airstrip was given an immediate start by the sum of twelve hundred and seventy-seven pounds donated by the island's twenty-five households. Seventy-five per cent of the cost of such strips was met by the Highlands and Islands Development Board, but the remainder still represented a substantial sum for a small community to raise.

Captain Whitfield recalls some avenues which were pursued in raising capital — such as tracing long-forgotten air ambulance funds from pre-National Health Service days. It was also discovered that other funds set up for whaling communities were lying dormant and forgotten and could be used for islands with whaling connections. The extent of these funds was usually small but every little counted.

The benefits of an airstrip on Foula were again illustrated on 25th December 1971. The island had been cut off by gales since 8th December with neither shipping nor aircraft being able to approach the island. On Christmas Day, however, a change in the wind encouraged Captain Whitfield to attempt a landing which he achieved, bringing in delayed mail and essential provisions.

Scheduled services, inaugurated between Sumburgh and Unst in 1970, were gradually expanded to include Lerwick, Fetlar, Whalsay and Fair Isle. Foula, Papa Stour and the shortest strip served by Loganair, the twelve hundred and fifty foot runway at Out Skerries, are served on a regular charter basis.

Captain Whitfield left Shetland to become Loganair's Chief Training Captain, based at Glasgow, in 1978. His work in the Shetlands saw the establishment of a chain of airstrips which brought new benefits of air travel and quick medical aid, through the availability of the air ambulance, to many individual communities. With the growth of oil-related activity in Shetland in the seventies he was involved not just in Loganair's own oil support flights, but also in building up a ground handling facility to cater for numerous other oil support aircraft operators who converged upon Shetland at that time.

Alan Whitfield's role in developing inter-island air travel in Shetland and in pioneering services to the most basic of strips, coupled with his numerous air ambulance mercy missions, was acknowledged in the award of the Queen's Commendation for Valuable Service in the Air in 1979. With over four hundred air ambulance flights performed during his flying career and with the distinction of having carried some of the most unusual passengers — such as some of the famous diminutive Shetland ponies — Captain Whitfield left Loganair on 30th December 1981 to return to his first love — the land. He now provides Ranger Services on behalf of the National Trust for Scotland amidst the dramatic scenery of Kintail.

The Traveller — Maisie Muir

If you are a business executive who travels a lot, you may think of yourself as a frequent flier. However, Loganair has one passenger who, it is suggested, outdoes all contenders for the record for most flights undertaken — and she does it without even leaving the Orkney Isles.

Maisie Muir operates the North Isles banking service for the Royal Bank of Scotland, a role which she has now performed for seventeen years. Miss Muir undertakes an average of five hundred and twenty-eight flights each year and by 1986 had exceeded nine thousand flights while performing this unique service since its inception in 1969.

From 1962 until 1969 the fore-runner of the Royal Bank of Scotland, the National Commercial Bank of Scotland, served the islands with their own yacht. A modest craft, it was known as the Otter Bank, and at most ports of call the bank's customers would come on board to transact their business. Now bank staff visit inner islands such as Shapinsay and Rousay using the regular ferry services.

Miss Muir, a native of Sanday, takes to the air to cover the North Isles. Westray gets two visits each week, while Sanday and Stronsay have banking services one day each week and the bank maintains its own premises on each of these islands. Other islands, Eday, Papa Westray and North Ronaldsay, have a visit once a month only and then banking business takes place in the informal surroundings of the home of one of the islanders.

A typical week for Miss Muir goes something like this:—

Monday	Kirkwall depart 1000 for Eday (or North Ronaldsay)
	Arrive 1705 back in Kirkwall
Tuesday	Kirkwall depart 1010 for Sanday (substituted once a month by
	Papa Westray)
	Arrive Kirkwall 1655
Wednesday	Kirkwall depart 0925 for Westray
	Arrive Kirkwall 1612
Thursday	Kirkwall depart 0925 for Stronsay
	Arrive Kirkwall 1610
Friday	Kirkwall depart 0925 for Westray
	Arrive Kirkwall 1612

Flying to work each day is no big drama for Maisie Muir. While she vividly recalls one particularly blustery day on Westray when five hefty islanders had to be recruited to hold down the wing of the aircraft when gale force winds threatened to topple it over as the engines were shut down, her journeys had been incident-free until 1st June 1984.

On that occasion mist closed in rapidly when the aircraft was descending on to the airstrip on Sanday. Missing the runway, the aircraft landed in the next field. Maisie was full of admiration for the poor pilot who negotiated several hazards while bringing the aircraft to a standstill. Said Maisie, "It all happened so quickly we could hardly tell what was going on, but luckily no one was hurt. It was over in seconds, leaving everyone only slightly shaken." For Maisie it was back to work as normal. (Loganair was unable to view this serious incident with the same sympathy as Maisie.)

There have been occasions when Kirkwall airport has been suddenly closed by fog preventing the aircraft from the North Isles returning to its home base. "I've had friends on such flights who have had to carry on to Wick or Inverness in order to land," said Maisie, "but I've not been so lucky and have always got home at night."

Strangely enough Maisie does not seem to experience looks of envy from her desk-bound colleagues in the main office in Kirkwall. "This job doesn't seem to attract colleagues who maybe have families or active social lives," says Maisie, "but I love it on the islands and to me this is a very special job."

The islands off the Orkney mainland also have other regular travellers, such as itinerant teachers, the school dentist and his assistant, the chiropodist, telephone engineers, etc. But without a doubt the Flying Banker is Loganair's most regular customer.

Maisie Muir — Orkney's flying banker   *Photo by Phoenix Photos, Kirkwall*

The Macphersons of Barra

When Katie Macpherson retired as Loganair's Station Manager on Barra in 1980 she completed an aviation career which had begun forty-four years earlier and had seen her serving a succession of five different airlines whilst still doing basically the same job. She is known by many on Barra as Katie Coddy, it being a nickname that she inherited from her father, the late John Macpherson (1876-1955).

Katie Macpherson gives a weather report to the pilot of an inbound flight while with BEA
Photo by courtesy of the RAF Museum, Hendon and British Airways

John Macpherson became known as The Coddy, when still a boy, through his activities in cod handline fishing. On leaving school The Coddy also participated in fishing for lobster and herring, but the entrepreneur in him saw him engage in other activities. He started his own merchant's business and in 1923 he became Postmaster at Northbay. Barra had few visitors until the late nineteen-twenties, but with the improvement in steamer services that situation began to change. The Coddy opened a boarding house to cater for the influx of tourists and he hired cars to the visitors, importing one of the very first cars to Barra, a Model T Ford. Cobles (small boats) were also rented to the visitors. He also represented the north part of Barra on Inverness County Council.

When Captain David Barclay was scouring the Hebrides for landing sites which could be used for the inauguration of regular air services to the islands he was about to admit defeat in Barra's case, having unsuccessfully combed the island for a suitable piece of ground. When Captain Barclay was telling him this, The Coddy replied, "Mmmmh! I was just thinking. Why don't you use the beach?" And so Barra's unique airport came into being.

The first air service to Barra commenced in 1936 and was operated by Northern and Scottish Airways Ltd, which later joined with Highland Airways Ltd to form Scottish Airways Ltd. Katie joined her father in running the "airfield". The Second World War disrupted regular air services, but Miss Macpherson recalls flying from Barra to Glasgow during wartime in an aircraft with the windows blacked out. Following the nationalisation of the independent airlines in 1947, Katie found herself in the employment of British European Airways, which in turn had joined with BOAC to form British Airways prior to the air services from Barra being passed over to Loganair in 1975.

Katie took charge of Barra's airfield in 1951 as Station Manager from her brother, Angus. Angus Macpherson had run the airfield for a short time following The Coddy's retiral. The special nature of the airfield made unique demands on Katie and she would often be seen on the wind-blown beach passing the latest assessment of weather and landing conditions over a hand radio to the approaching aircraft. Her special qualities were all-important for the successful operation of many air ambulance flights, a service which sadly she herself was to have experience of in February 1980 when she suffered a stroke not long after her retiral.

Although shy and modest, Miss Macpherson could not avoid being in the public eye and there was no escaping the recognition that was her due. In 1969 she was awarded the MBE for her part in keeping Barra in touch with the world and the world in touch with Barra. Another accolade came in the form of the Woman of the Year Award.

There is no doubting the unique contribution made by the Macpherson family to life in Barra, but The Coddy left another lasting contribution. John Macpherson was a great Gaelic folklorist earning acclaim from far beyond the shores of Barra and making him a popular fear-an-taighe to his boarding house guests. Much of the Gaelic oral tradition has now been lost, but fortunately many of The Coddy's tales were recorded and can still be enjoyed.

For the Record

Loganair does not operate the world's fastest passenger airliner, the BAC/Aerospatiale Concorde, or the aircraft with the greatest passenger-carrying capability, the Boeing 747.

It does not come close to challenging Aeroflot of the Soviet Union for the title of world's largest airline, or Pan-Am for their record for the longest non-stop scheduled flight, the seven thousand four hundred and seventy-five mile hop from Sydney to San Francisco by Boeing 747SP in thirteen hours and twenty-five minutes.

The oldest person to fly was Mr. Shigechiyo Izumi who flew from Tokunashima Island to Tokyo in his one-hundred-and-ninth year. But Loganair does not operate that route so no claim to fame there either. However, while its type of operation does not even put it into the periphery of some of these, Loganair does have a few unique features all of its own which are worth recording.

Shortest Scheduled Flight in the World

Loganair's service between the Orcadian islands of Westray and Papa Westray, with a timetabled duration of only two minutes, is documented by the famous Guinness Book of Records as the shortest scheduled flight by fixed-wing aircraft in the world.

However, with a favourable head-wind the journey often takes little over one minute. The record time for the flight is fifty-eight seconds, accomplished on a flight under the command of Captain Andrew D Alsop.

This service, part of the Orkney Islands internal air network, was inaugurated in September 1967 and has been operated with Britten-Norman Islander aircraft since that time. The distance flown on this unique hop is a mere one-and-a-half miles and passengers can see the windsock at their destination while still sitting on the ground at the airfield of their departure.

Longest Runway in Scotland

Since 1977 Loganair has been the only airline to operate a scheduled service utilising Scotland's longest runway, that being the year in which it took over the operation of the Glasgow—Campbeltown route from the previous incumbent, British Airways.

Campbeltown is served by the RAF airfield at Machrihanish where runway 30/12 has a length of ten thousand and three feet. This exceeds the maximum runway lengths at major Scottish airports such as Prestwick (nine thousand eight hundred feet), Glasgow (eight thousand seven hundred and twenty feet) and Edinburgh (eight thousand four hundred feet).

By way of comparison, the length of the runway at Machrihanish also exceeds the distance flown by Loganair on the world's shortest scheduled route between Westray and Papa Westray.

First Airline in the World

In 1966 Loganair ordered its first Britten-Norman Islander aircraft and when the airline took delivery the following year it became the first airline in the world to operate the type.

The Islander is ideally suited to the small unsophisticated airstrips such as serve many remote communities as it requires little over six hundred feet for take-off. Loganair continues to operate several Islanders in 1987. The aircraft continues as a workhorse on the internal services of the Orkney and Shetland Islands as well as on some of the thinner density mainland routes. Three Islanders are on permanent standby as Air Ambulance aircraft, based at Glasgow, Kirkwall and Lerwick.

The Britten-Norman Islander aircraft continues to be a worldwide best-seller with over a thousand now sold. While its name is highly appropriate to the Loganair routes on which it serves, the Islander recalls its place of original manufacture at Bembridge on the Isle of Wight.

Longest Scheduled Flight within Scotland

Loganair took the record for the longest non-stop airlink within Scotland when it started the service from Edinburgh to Lerwick in 1979. The two-hour flight, inaugurated with the DHC Twin Otter aircraft carrying eighteen passengers, saw the introduction of in-flight catering to Loganair's scheduled services.

At Lerwick Loganair uses Tingwall Airport, only two miles from town, in preference to the larger Sumburgh Airport twenty-five miles away, for this and the other Shetland services. In 1981 the Edinburgh—Lerwick service was extended to continue on to the island of Unst.

Serving the Far North

As part of its Shetland Isles internal network, Loganair operates scheduled services to the island of Unst. This airfield was built by the army in 1968 at Baltasound and is the most northerly in the British Isles. The lighthouse at Muckle Flugga, a rock lying off the northern tip of the island, is the northernmost inhabited point in the United Kingdom. Unst is a breeding place for the Great Skua, making the island of particular interest to ornithologists.

In 1981 Loganair's Edinburgh—Lerwick service was extended to Unst. The airstrip has a tarred runway two thousand one hundred feet in length and is now administered by the Shetland Isles Islands Council. Unst airstrip was extended in 1978 enabling it to undertake a strategic role as a transit point for traffic bound for the northern oilfields of the North Sea.

'Times subject to Tides'

Loganair is the sole operator to the only airstrip in the United Kingdom where schedules are shown as "subject to tides". Aircraft visiting the Isle of Barra land on Tràigh Mhòr (literally 'Great Shore') where the cockle strand provides a firm surface at low tide for take-offs and landings.

Loganair has flown into Barra since the early nineteen-sixties and has served Barra regularly since 1975 when it took over the service there from Glasgow from British Airways. During the winter Tiree is an intermediate stop on this service. 1975 also saw the introduction of the Western Isles inter-island service connecting Barra, Benbecula and Stornoway.

Aircraft have in fact been a familiar sight on Barra for many years. The first Glasgow—Barra service was inaugurated by Captain David Barclay for Northern and Scottish Airways Ltd in 1936, following the licensing of the airstrip by the Air Ministry on 7th August of that year. The aircraft then used was one of the legendary De Havilland Rapides, a twin-engined bi-plane which was to be the mainstay of several Scottish airlines in the nineteen-thirties.

Ambulance flights have been known to land at Barra during the night, but only under ideal conditions and with flares being used to aid touch-down. Aircraft are unable to land within three hours either side of high tide and this gives an indication of the flexibility required for flights. This can be highlighted in winter when high tide may be at noon, but daylight lasts from only 8.30am until 3.30pm.

The airfield at Barra is operated by Loganair and in this role it is responsible for all the facilities there including the aerodrome's fire tender. Barra airfield is equipped with a modern terminal building which Loganair opened in June 1978.

A Breath of Fresh Air

In 1979 Loganair became the first airline to place a complete ban on in-flight smoking (with the full support of the smokers among their team of pilots and executives).

The advantages of discouraging the habit on small aircraft with confined cabin space are perhaps obvious. However, Loganair has managed to maintain this policy even with the introduction of larger aircraft on its routes, giving a lead to larger airlines and earning commendation from organisations such as the anti-smoking group ASH (Action on Smoking and Health).

"Air Born"

Loganair is believed to hold the record for the most babies born in-flight. (Any other claimants please contact the author!) Its Air Ambulance duties mean that it flies expectant mothers who have to make a dash by air from remote locations to a city hospital.

However, over the years some babies have decided that even the speed of flight is not quite enough to allow them to make their arrival into the world in the conventional surroundings of a hospital. Loganair takes the arrival of babies, while several thousand feet above the ground, all in its stride and has also established a tradition of presenting each of them with an inscribed silver goblet to commemorate the event. In-flight births are registered with the Civil Aviation Authority, who are reported to be a little curious about flights which arrive at their destination with more passengers on board than at the point of origin.

Loganair's first "air born" delivery was that of Katy Ferguson Leynair Devin on 2nd August 1973 while two thousand feet above Kirkwall. The event, which took place on board Islander G-AWNR flying from Stronsay to Aberdeen, was commemorated by Mr and Mrs Devin when choosing a name for their daughter. The name 'Leynair' was created from the last syllable of the name of the pilot, Captain Jamie Bayley, and the last syllable of Loganair.

When Jonathan Ayres was born en route from Islay to Glasgow on 6th January 1982, his surname seemed purpose made to mark his birth at two thousand feet above Houston in some way. His parents named him Jonathan Philip Logan Ayres.

There have been many coincidences surrounding births in the air. At one stage it seemed that in-flight births were to be the preserve of baby girls with the little ladies accounting for the first six such events. Baby Donald Swanson changed that when he entered the world seven thousand feet above the Kyles of Bute whilst his mother was being whisked from Islay to Glasgow.

In January 1982 there were no less than three in-flight deliveries within forty-eight hours, an amazing sequence considering that a whole year often passes without a single delivery while airborne. The first baby was Annaliese Harding, born above Fraserburgh while en route from Lerwick to Aberdeen. Weighing-in at only 2lb 1oz, Annaliese was in a critical condition for some time, but all ended happily when she returned to Shetland three months later, fit and well. Next came Sarah Jane MacDonald while flying from Campbeltown to Glasgow to be followed by Jonathan Ayres on his flight from Islay to Glasgow — both births taking place with the same pilot at the controls, Captain Dave Dyer.

The likelihood of twins being born in the air must be fairly minimal but that did not discourage David and Lynsey Henderson, probably the only twins to be born forty miles apart. Their mum was being flown from Lerwick to Aberdeen on Friday 13th August 1982 when Lynsey decided to make an appearance while the aircraft was still thirty miles north of Fraserburgh. David followed his sister into the world just as the aircraft reached Dyce airport.

The arrival of Stuart James Eunson on 27th January 1985, en route from Lerwick to Aberdeen, marked Loganair's fourteenth "air born" delivery — and Amanda Lesley McAlpine chose the same route exactly fifteen months later to become the fifteenth.

World's Largest Trislander Operator

Loganair became the largest operator in the world of the Britten-Norman Trislander, having eight of this type of aircraft in its fleet at one stage.

The Trislander was a development of the rugged and already highly successful Islander. While retaining many of the physical characteristics of the Islander, the Trislander fuselage had a length of 14.8 metres (compared with the Islander's length of 11 metres) increasing Loganair's normal payload of eight passengers with the Islander to sixteen passengers in the Trislander. A unique characteristic, from which this aircraft took its name, was the inclusion of a third engine high in the tail.

The Trislander requires a take-off run of only twelve hundred and ninety feet which has made it a practical proposition for many of Scotland's more basic airstrips while giving an increased capacity. On scheduled services the Trislander first appeared on the Dundee—Glasgow route following delivery of the initial aircraft in 1973. The last aircraft was finally ousted from the Stornoway—Benbecula—Barra service in 1982 by the larger DHC Twin Otter.

Most Scheduled Destinations

Loganair serves more destinations in the United Kingdom than any other airline, a situation which has now prevailed for several years.

At the time of preparation of this book Loganair was serving twenty-eight points on its network. Nearest contenders were British Airways serving eighteen destinations in the United Kingdom, followed by Air UK with fifteen. Next came Air Ecosse and Dan-Air, each serving fourteen UK airports, while British Midland Airways had thirteen points on its UK network.

While all airlines' schedules are constantly changing with the addition of new routes and occasionally the relinquishing of others, Loganair's lead is such that it seems unlikely to be challenged in the foreseeable future.

First Flight to Glasgow

Having pioneered new airfields over a wide range of locations throughout Scotland, Loganair was the first operator to land on many.

However, Loganair was also the first airline to land at what quickly became Scotland's busiest airport — Glasgow. The site had originally been established as an RAF station in 1932. It was later transferred to the Royal Navy as Royal Naval Air Station HMS "Sanderling" and was finally closed in 1963.

The City of Glasgow Corporation acquired the airfield and it was officially opened on Monday 2nd May 1966, replacing Renfrew Airport. On the afternoon of Sunday 1st May Captain Ken Foster, at the controls of Loganair's Cherokee 6 aircraft, flew low over the new airport checking the landing lights and markers on behalf of the Ministry of Aviation and then gently touched down at the deserted airport. (BEA made their first landing later that evening in a Dart Herald which, like Loganair's Cherokee, flew in from nearby Renfrew.)

Loganair established their Head Office at Glasgow Airport at this time and their subsequent growth has been conducted from this base.

Red and white check of the early seventies gave way to a black and red outfit *Photos by Randak Design*
M.D. Scott Grier with some of the airline's beauties in their 1984 uniforms *Photo by Bob Nicholson*

Aircraft Names

The People Behind the Names

From the time that Loganair first commenced operating air ambulance flights, the airline maintained a tradition of naming the ambulance aircraft in its Britten-Norman Islander fleet.

The names which these aircraft bear are mostly of individuals who have made a specific contribution to the air ambulance service either directly or indirectly and it is not surprising to find the names of many of the pioneers of Scottish civil aviation honoured on Loganair's aircraft.

From time to time aircraft are sold from the fleet to be replaced by newer counterparts. The names have then been transferred to the new aircraft whenever possible.

In addition to the names which follow, Loganair also operated a Vickers Viscount leased from British Air Ferries during Winter 1983/84 which bore the name "The Flying Scotsman".

Sister Jean Kennedy

The names of those
who in their lives fought for life,
Who wore at their hearts
the fire's centre.
Born of the sun,
they travelled a short while
towards the sun
And left the vivid air
signed with their honour.

Stephen Spender

Photo by courtesy of John Kennedy

Sister Jean Kennedy, who originally came from the Isle of Coll, had already participated in over two hundred mercy flights with the Air Ambulance Service when a message was sent to her at Glasgow's Southern General Hospital requesting her assistance on the night of 28th September 1957.

67

The emergency call was from the Isle of Islay where a shepherd's wife, Mrs Margaret McClugash, was seriously ill with diabetes. The distress call was answered by De Havilland Heron G-AOFY and Sister Kennedy joined Captain T N Calderwood and Radio Officer Hugh McGinlay at Renfrew Airport.

However, G-AOFY was not to fulfil its mission, crashing in bad weather and low cloud only three-quarters of a mile from touch-down at Islay's Glenegedale Airport. Sister Kennedy, Captain Calderwood and Radio Officer McGinlay were all dead when would-be rescuers reached the mangled wreckage of the Heron.

A second Heron was prepared for take-off at Renfrew Airport under the command of Captain Eric Starling, First Officer Maclean and a colleague of Sister Kennedy, Sister Isobel Thomson. It was dawn when the second aircraft was able to combat the severe weather and uplift Mrs McClugash from Islay. It must have been no easy task for this crew setting out with the knowledge of the tragedy which had overcome their colleagues a few hours earlier; the anguish of the worst night in the history of the Air Ambulance Service was not to be eased any with the knowledge that the patient would be the better as a result of the mercy flight — for Mrs McClugash died as the aircraft was approaching Renfrew.

It is tragic that those on board G-AOFY should have been killed while on a mission to save life, but it is typical of the people who have manned the air ambulances over the years that they are prepared to hazard extremely adverse weather conditions when every minute may be critical to an ailing patient. Sister Kennedy had been flying with the air ambulance service for five years, a volunteer as are all the nurses.

It could therefore be seen as a tribute to all the nurses for the sacrifices they make, as well as to Sister Jean Kennedy for her ultimate sacrifice, when British European Airways named one of their remaining De Havilland Herons after her. The Herons are now gone, but Sister Kennedy is still remembered with Loganair carrying on the tradition with one of their Britten-Norman Islanders.

A cairn erected in Renfrew, close to the site of the former Renfrew Airport, pays tribute to all the airmen and nurses who served the Scottish Air Ambulance Service from 1933 until the airport closed in 1966. A separate plaque on the cairn pays homage to Captain Calderwood, Radio Officer McGinlay and Sister Kennedy.

E L Gandar Dower Esq   *Photo by courtesy of Captain Eric Starling*

E L Gandar Dower Esq.

When Eric Gandar Dower graduated from Oxford University his ambition was an acting career. Indeed he formed his own touring company, but with his family against such a career this was all taking place without their knowledge. During one theatrical tour, however, an act of heroism in saving a boy from drowning captured the interest of the newspapers. The resultant publicity also drew his family's attention to his secret acting career and soon an ultimatum followed — family or theatre.

Gandar Dower therefore reluctantly gave up the stage and turned his attention to investigating the possibilities of setting up a flying school at Aberdeen in March 1931. It was during the pursuit of this adventure that he realised the advantages that air travel could bring in the north of Scotland. For example, the rail journey from Aberdeen to Caithness took eight hours compared with fifty minutes by aircraft, while the onward ferry journey to Orkney required two-and-a-half hours over sometimes inhospitable waters while it could be flown in fifteen minutes. Aberdeen to Shetland took an hour and thirty-five minutes to fly while the steamer took eighteen hours and could be stormbound in port for days in winter.

Aberdeen Airways was set up on 2nd January 1934. Ground was levelled at Dyce for an airstrip and all services had to be laid on too — the village of Dyce had its first electricity supply because Gandar Dower had to have electric power laid on for the airfield. In a radio interview recorded in 1974 Gandar Dower recalled how the public was slow to adapt to air travel — the first week of operations cost four hundred and fifty pounds while the total fares paid by the the three passengers to travel came to eight pounds and fifteen shillings! How things have changed is shown by the modern and busy Aberdeen Airport of today which occupies the site of Gandar Dower's original airfield.

From a service twice a week to Glasgow, the airline gradually grew. An Aberdeen—Wick—Thurso—Orkney service was inaugurated in May 1935 and this was followed by an Aberdeen—Edinburgh service. In June 1936 the Aberdeen—Orkney service was extended to Shetland and in 1937, in order to make the airline sound less parochial, the name was changed from Aberdeen Airways to Allied Airways (Gandar Dower) Ltd.

This was appropriate for on 12th July, in a far-sighted move, a link was forged from Newcastle to Stavanger, under the command of the Chief Pilot, Captain Eric Starling. The route was flown with a De Havilland DH86B Express Air Liner, G-AETM — 'The Norseman'. The sleek four-engined bi-plane made the journey five times per week and carried ten passengers.

At the outset of operations Gandar Dower had bought a bus to transport passengers from Aberdeen to the airfield. At that time, as he recalled in 1974, a small car would have been adequate and they would have been happy to pick up passengers at their doors in order to get their custom. By 1939, however, it looked as if the years of struggle had been worthwhile and the airline was sufficiently established to look forward to a prosperous future. But World War Two was to dash such hopes. Then in 1947 Allied Airways was nationalised along with the other independent airlines and, like his rival and fellow pioneer Captain E E Fresson, E L Gandar Dower was given totally inadequate credit for the foundations he had laid and the airline that he had built up from the ground. Gandar Dower fought the take-over vigorously for many years.

Gandar Dower did retain three of his Dragon Rapides following the transfer of Allied Airways to BEA. These aircraft operated under the name of 'E L Gandar Dower' and were used for charter operations from Aberdeen until 1950.

One of these aircraft, DH89 Dragon Rapide G-ADAH then appropriately named 'Pioneer', remained at Dyce until 1966. This aircraft is now preserved, in the livery of Allied Airways (Gandar Dower) Ltd, at the Museum of Flight at East Fortune, near North Berwick in East Lothian. The museum has a limited opening season and enquiries about possible viewing times may be made by telephoning (062 088) 308.

Dragon Rapide G-ADAH, 'The Thurso Venturer', of Allied Airways (Gandar Dower) Ltd
Photo by courtesy of Captain Eric Starling

Sir James Young Simpson

Sir James Young Simpson is another notable after whom British European Airways named one of their De Havilland Heron aircraft and Loganair continued the tradition. Simpson, however, was from a different era from those others similarly honoured, being born on 7th June 1811 at Bathgate, Linlithgowshire (later West Lothian), the seventh son of a local baker.

While Sir James Young Simpson's career took place long before the advent of modern air travel and air ambulance flights, there are many patients today who still appreciate the benefits of his work.

James Young Simpson studied medicine at the University of Edinburgh, obtaining his MD in 1832. He became Professor of Obstetrics at the University in 1840.

In 1846 William Thomas Morton demonstrated the use of ether as a general anaesthetic to a gathering of physicians at Massachusetts General Hospital. News of Morton's findings soon reached Europe and Simpson first experimented with the method in obstetrics on 19th January 1847. He then conducted further experiments both upon himself and his assistants with other vapours in order to discover a general anaesthetic.

On 4th November 1847 James Young Simpson substituted chloroform for ether with complete success. But his use of chloroform attracted opposition from other obstetricians, and from the clergy who held the view that pain was an integral part of the childbirth process. In 1853, however, Queen Victoria used chloroform during the birth of Prince Leopold and from that point on the anaesthetic gained general acceptance.

James Young Simpson became physician to the Queen in Scotland in 1847 and he was created a baronet in 1866. He founded gynaecology by his sound tests and he developed the long obstetrics forceps that are named after him. He introduced iron wire sutures and acupressure, a method of arresting haemorrhage. He also made great contributions to hospital reform.

Simpson's work with chloroform was published in his "Account of a New Anaesthetic Agent" and other works included "Obstetric Memoirs and Contributions" and "Acupressure". Writings on medical history paid particular attention to leprosy in Scotland. Outwith the world of medicine Simpson was particularly interested in archaeology and this interest is reflected in his work "Archaeological Essays".

Sir James Young Simpson died in London on 6th May, 1870.

Sir James Young Simpson
Photo by National Galleries of Scotland

Extracts from Captain Barclay's Log

RECORD OF FLIGHTS.

689. 15

Date.	Aircraft. Type.	Reg. No.	Journey.	Time in Air. Hrs.	Min.	Remarks.
5.2.36	—	G-ACMO	Renfrew Brought forward …	—	20	
5.2.36	DH 84	G-ACFG	Renfrew - Skye S. Uist - Barra S. Uist. Skye. Renfrew	6	30	X
8.2.36						
11.2.36	—	G-ACMO	Renfrew - Renfrew	1		R/T. N/S. Returned Dud engine.
11.2.36	—	G-ACFG	Renfrew - Skye n. Uist. Barra S. Uist. Skye. Renfrew	3	55	X R/T + N/T.
14.2.36	Martin Cruiser	G-ACMO	Renfrew. Local	—	40	Engine Test
19.2.36		G-ACYL	" "	1	—	
			Carried forward …	702	50	

5 February 1936   The first flight to include a landing at Barra. A second flight on 11th February turned back due to engine trouble and then proceeded with an alternative machine. The first aircraft has a test flight on 14th February after repairs have been completed.

RECORD OF FLIGHTS.

Date.	Aircraft. Type.	Reg. No.	Journey.	Time in Air. Hrs.	Min.	Remarks.
			Brought forward …	572	10	
16.9.35	DH 84	G-ACFG	Inverness - Dornoch	—	20	Lord & Lady London derry + landing.
" "	—	—	Dornoch - Inverness	—	25	
" "		—	Inverness - Renfrew	1	45	
30.9.35	DH 87A	G-ADBF	Local	—	20	
1.10.35	DH 87A	G-ADDF	"	—	15	
2.10.35	DH 84	G-ACJS	Renfrew - Islay	2	25	
3.10.35	DH 84	G-ACMC	" Local	—	20	Wireless Test.
4.10.35	DH 84	G-ACJS	Renfrew TIREE	1	05	TIREE
" "	" "		TIREE - RENFREW	1	—	Beach Landing
		G-TTT BAY	Beach Landing Carried forward …	580	25	6 A.M.

4 October 1935   First landing at Tiree undertaken at 6.00am to take advantage of low tide on the beach. A flight on 16th September for Lord and Lady Londonderry to Dornoch is one of the many flights for well-known personages of the time. Other flights included trips to Balmoral for King George V.

Date.	AIRCRAFT. Type.	Markings.	Captain.	Engines.	Holder's Operating Capacity.	Journey or Nature of Flight. From	To	Departure.	Arrival.	FLYING TIMES. DAY. In Charge.	Second.	NIGHT. In Charge.	Second.	Instrument Flying.	REMARKS.
									10,6	47:07	30:03	172:25	3:45	255:27	TOTALS Brought Forward
1950															
11.11.50	DH 89	G-AGUR	Self	GD. VHF. MF	P.1	Renfrew	Tiree	1200	1305	1:05	—	—	—	—	Ambulance
"	"	"	"	"	"	Tiree	Barra	1315	1345	:30	—	—	—	—	1 Pab. 1H - Ren.
"	"	"	"	"	"	Barra	Renfrew	1355	1605	1:10	—	—	—	—	
18.4.50	DH 89	G-AGUP	"	"	"	Renfrew	Islay	1345	1435	:50	—	—	—	—	Ambulance 1 Pab Ros - I
"	"	"	"	"	"	Islay	Benbecula	1438	1633	:55	—	—	—	—	1 Pab. 1U - Ren.
"	"	"	"	"	"	Benbecula	Renfrew	1604	1910	—	—	3:06	—	3:06	Both engines icing. N.F. Saw engine
21.11.50	"	G-AGUR	"	"	"	Renfrew	Renfrew	1530	1605	—	:35	—	—	—	dist. H.O. Coldenwood
23.11.50	"	G-AGUR	"	"	"	Renfrew	C'town	1245	1320	:35	—	—	—	—	Ambulance
28.11.50	"	G-AGUR	"	"	"	C'town	Renfrew	1340	1415	:35	—	—	—	—	1 Pab. cc - Ren
18.11.50	"	G-AGUR	"	"	"	Renfrew	C'town	0930	1010	:40	—	—	—	—	S.C. Service.
"	"	"	"	"	"	C'town	Renfrew	1025	1105	:40	—	—	—	—	No Returns.
									10,6	54:07	30:38	175:31	3:45	258:33	TOTALS Carried Forward

18 November 1950   The flight from Benbecula in which the De Havilland Rapide suffered icing problems during extreme weather conditions and resulted in the introduction of the De Havilland Herons to the BEA fleet.   The cryptic note "N.F." could mean anything from a jocular "not fun" to a more serious "No Fuel" or even "near fatal".

Captain David Barclay, MBE, OStJ

The name of Captain David Barclay is legendary in the Hebrides for his air ambulance flights in all weathers over a period of thirty years and also for pioneering aviation in the islands. However, the son of a Greenock dairyman, David Barclay appeared destined for a career in farming, but it was the influence of his brother which was to see him follow a different course.

Malcolm Barclay started taking flying lessons at Beardmore's Flying School in 1927 and David enthusiastically gleaned the rudiments of flying as he watched his brother progress. On 12th December 1927 the Scottish Flying Club was founded and Malcolm ensured that David was signed up as a founder member, No. 31, despite protests that the family dairy business would not allow him time to fly. But after only four hours and twenty-five minutes of dual instruction David Barclay had set a new record when he made his first solo flight. In April 1928, at the age of 23, he gained his Royal Aero Club Aviator's Certificate.

Subsequently flying took place as often as David Barclay could afford it, but at thirty shillings an hour he decided that it would be a better arrangement if someone else paid him to fly. He therefore joined the RAF in 1929 and served in India from 1930 until 1934. There Captain Barclay had read about the work that Midland and Scottish Air Ferries had done in pioneering flights from Renfrew to Campbeltown and Islay and he had already decided that the next step in his career would take him to the islands off the west coast of Scotland.

In 1934, flying for Midland and Scottish Air Ferries, Captain Barclay undertook his first air ambulance flight and on 5th December he flew the inaugural flight of Northern and Scottish Airways from Renfrew to Skye in DH84 Dragon Moth G-ACFG.

In January of the following year Captain Barclay inaugurated an extension of the service to South Uist and in March 1936 he flew the first regular service into North Uist, landing at Sollas. Connecting services were supplied on demand to Barra, Benbecula and Harris, but the service was a flexible one and the order of stops was frequently changed to suit the passengers.

The islanders were initially sceptical of flying and indeed a seventy-year-old patient from Benbecula insisted on making out his will before being put on board the aircraft. He arrived safe and sound in Glasgow and became an enthusiastic convert to air travel. If some showed a little reticence towards flying as passengers themselves, they nevertheless quickly realised its value in transporting goods speedily from the mainland whether it be a spare part for a car, batteries for a radio set, or food supplies if the steamer had been detained.

A flight from Turnhouse to the Orkneys on 19th April 1940, during the Second World War, almost saw the end of Captain Barclay's flying career and indeed of Captain Barclay himself. He was flying an Army General and his aides in Dragon G-ACNG, an aircraft which had a temperamental streak in it. On arrival over Orkney the aircraft became nose-heavy and despite efforts to correct it, it decided to take a forty-five degree plunge into the runway at Hatston Aerodrome.

Captain David Barclay   *Photo by courtesy of Captain Eric Starling*

The impact destroyed the front of the aircraft, Captain Barclay miraculously surviving, but sustaining injuries including a smashed pelvis and ankle, broken ribs, a fractured nose, plus facial cuts and bruising all over his body. He was hospitalised in Kirkwall for two-and-a-half months and his chances of walking again looked slim. However, a combination of skilful surgery in rebuilding the shattered ankle plus the dogged determination of Captain Barclay himself saw him not only on his feet again but also, after a few months back in the air.

The injuries did, however, limit Captain Barclay's aeronautical ability a little in terms of the aircraft he could fly. When BEA was formed after the war the DC-3, or Dakota, appeared on many Scottish routes. Captain Barclay could handle this larger aircraft under normal conditions, but with reduced power in his right foot the aircraft made exceptional demands when put into emergency procedures such as flight with an engine out of action. The effects of the injury therefore effectively confined him to the smaller aircraft types.

Captain Barclay had another grim flight in a Rapide in November 1950. An outbound flight from Renfrew to Benbecula had been uneventful taking the normal one hour and forty-five minutes. However, the weather had changed by the return journey, severe icing and a strong head-wind forcing the aircraft down to thirty-three hundred feet leaving an uncomfortably narrow safety margin for crossing the mountains of Argyll. Difficulties were experienced in getting a radio bearing and it was probably due to luck as well as skill that the flight was completed in three hours and six minutes with fuel for twenty minutes left. As a result, Captain Barclay put forward a strong case for a more sophisticated aircraft with de-icing equipment. The aircraft which he had in mind was the twin-engined De Havilland Dove, but he came away with one even better, the four-engined De Havilland Heron which could comfortably maintain a height of six-and-a-half thousand feet with a full load with one engine shut down.

Captain Barclay retired with an overwhelming send-off on 30th April 1965. His final flight was a scheduled run with a Heron from Barra and Tiree to Renfrew and islanders turned out at both airfields to say their personal goodbyes. Laden with gifts, Captain Barclay arrived back at Renfrew twenty-five minutes late — but there were no complaints. Indeed it was an appropriate send-off for the man who had flown about three thousand of the five-and-a-half thousand air ambulance flights which had been carried out up until that time, and in all weather conditions.

Through a flying career which was nearly all performed without leaving Scotland, Captain Barclay had logged one-and-a-half million miles and eighteen thousand flying hours when he retired. David Barclay died at the age of 75 in February 1981.

**Captain David Barclay visits Islay at the end of an illustrious flying career
for the unveiling of a plaque in his honour**   *Photo by courtesy of Ian Harper*

Captain E E Fresson, OBE

The exploits of Edmund Fresson in China during the period up to and following the First World War make an adventure story of their own. However, it is the services which he rendered in establishing civil aviation in the north of Scotland that make him one of the great unsung heroes of the pioneering days.

Having returned to the United Kingdom in 1927, Captain Fresson spent his time giving joy-riding flights at venues throughout the UK which gradually made their way further north. During one such tour in 1931 he carried the first fare-paying passenger to Kirkwall from Wick and immediately realised the potential of a scheduled air service where the only other means of transport between the Orkneys and the mainland was a long sea passage over unpredictable waters.

In 1933 he formed Highland Airways Ltd and the first scheduled flight took place on 8th May from Inverness to Wick and Kirkwall with a four-passenger twin-engined ST4 Monospar monoplane named "Inverness" (G-ACEW). On 2nd August an eight-seater DH84 Dragon aircraft was introduced and, despite the absence of sophisticated navigation equipment, the first flights, on a charter basis, were made northwards over the open expanses of the North Sea to the Shetlands.

The following year saw further pioneering with the opening of a scheduled service from Aberdeen to Kirkwall on 7th May 1934 and experimental flights between Inverness and Stornoway. On 30th May over two thousand letters were carried from Inverness to Kirkwall with twelve thousand letters being carried on the return flight — the first internal air mail service in Britain had been inaugurated.

Captain Fresson's airline grew further in 1935 with the arrival of a DH89 Rapide aircraft and on 3rd June 1936 his service from Aberdeen to Sumburgh in Shetland was started.

In 1937 Highland Airways joined with the Renfrew-based Northern and Scottish Airways to form Scottish Airways, but Captain Fresson's base at Inverness retained autonomy to concentrate on the northern routes while the Renfrew division under George Nicholson was the base for operations to the islands off Scotland's western seaboard. Captain Fresson continued operations throughout the Second World War, his knowledge of the Northern Isles being invaluable to the military authorities during that period. 1944 saw the commencement of the air service from Inverness to Stornoway after numerous delays in agreeing landing arrangements at Stornoway.

On 1st February 1947 Scottish Airways was nationalised with the creation of British European Airways. In the months that followed Captain Fresson was to see his knowledge, gained from many years of pioneering work, being ignored by the new BEA officials, the introduction of unsuitable aircraft on the Northern Isles routes and a small profitable operation being turned into a loss-maker. As had happened to some other pioneers following the nationalisation of their airlines, Captain Fresson was unceremoniously dismissed by BEA. This was in 1948 and Captain Fresson then set off for a new life in Kenya.

Captain Fresson was regarded with particular affection in the Orkney Islands where his air services brought many new amenities to isolated communities. On the island of North Ronaldsay air links were introduced following a public meeting which resulted in the construction of a make-shift airstrip by sixty islanders, with the aid of twenty handcarts, within a day. The lead given by the people of North Ronaldsay was followed by the populations of other smaller islands such as Westray, Sanday and Stronsay.

It was the ability to operate into these simple airstrips and often into suitable fields that gave rise to the realisation that an air ambulance service was feasible. Highland Airways were contracted by Orkney County Council to provide the air ambulance service in October 1933, only two months after commencing their first scheduled service. Urgent cases were usually flown to Kirkwall's Balfour Hospital and many lives were saved due to the advantage that the air ambulance had over traditional methods of transport from the outlying islands.

One memorable flight was piloted by Captain John Hankins on a wild night in 1939. A skilful landing was made after dark on a three-hundred-yard field on the Isle of Sanday, the only illumination being provided by car headlights, in order to take an urgent case to hospital.

Services to the islands lying off the Orcadian mainland did not fit in with the plans of the newly nationalised BEA and in many ways much of Captain Fresson's work in the Orkneys was pioneered by Loganair all over again when it arrived to set up inter-island scheduled air services and the all-important air ambulance service twenty years later. However Captain Fresson's services to the Orkneys are not forgotten by the islanders who unveiled a memorial to him at Kirkwall Airport in 1976.

The inauguration of the Orkney air mail service is intimated by the 1934 poster
Photo by courtesy of Captain Eric Starling

Captain Eric A Starling, FRMetS

Eric Starling began his career in aviation when he joined the Herts and Essex Gliding Club in 1930. He gained his Aviator's Certificate the following year at the age of nineteen, qualifying to fly an aircraft before taking his examination to operate more conventional transport, the motor car.

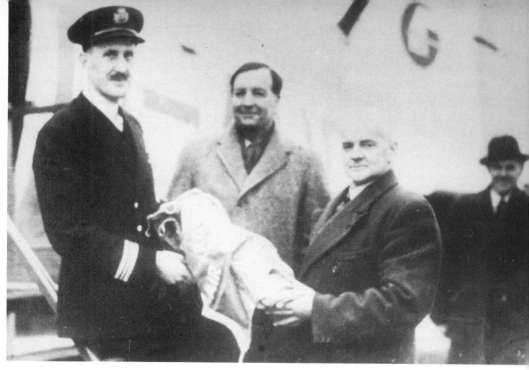

Captains Starling *left* **and Fresson** *centre* **at the start of the Inverness—Stornoway air mail service**
Captain Starling's Aviator's Certificate No 10213 *Photos by courtesy of Captain Eric Starling*

He joined E L Gandar Dower as Chief Pilot of Aberdeen Airways at its inception in 1934 and he was responsible for surveying routes for the airline to Glasgow, Stromness and Shetland from Aberdeen, and from Newcastle to Stavanger. Captain Starling flew the inaugural flight in the sleek DH86B Express Air Liner from Newcastle to Stavanger on 12th July 1937. Passengers could link on to this service from Edinburgh, Perth and London with flights by North Eastern Airways and upon arrival at Stavanger they could connect on to Oslo with DNL (Norwegian Airlines). The six days a week service endures today, but is now operated by the BAe 146 jet aircraft of Dan-Air.

Captain Starling also flew the first flight from Aberdeen to Shetland inaugurating the first regular air mail on 2nd June 1936, which he recalls as being 'a bit naughty'. Captain Fresson of Highland Airways, rival of Aberdeen Airways (by this time renamed Allied Airways (Gandar Dower) Ltd), had been the driving force in preparing the airfield at Sumburgh Head and had planned his inaugural flight for the following day when the DH84 Dragon Moth of Allied Airways arrived unannounced. Early acknowledgement was given of his services in the naming of Allied Airways DH84 Dragon Moth G-ACAN "Starling".

During the Second World War Captain Starling commanded No 3 Ferry Training Unit, No 292 Squadron, RAF Stations Jessore and Agatala while serving in the Royal Air Force Coastal Command.

Upon termination of hostilities, Captain Starling joined Scottish Airways Ltd (which had been formed in 1937 through the combining of Northern and Scottish Airways Ltd

Captain Eric Starling poses before a Shorts Scion of Aberdeen Airways
Photo by courtesy of Captain Eric Starling

and Highland Airways Ltd) at Inverness. Following the nationalisation of the independent airlines Captain Starling continued with British European Airways, moving to Renfrew.

On 16th February 1948 Eric Starling piloted the first air mail service from Inverness to Stornoway, and on 1st April 1949 he flew a DC-3 on BEA's inaugural flight from Edinburgh Turnhouse to London. From 1949 until 1968 he was Flight Manager — Scotland for BEA. During this period he was heavily involved in the Scottish Air Ambulance Service, in addition to BEA's other activities in Scotland, and he frequently piloted air ambulance flights.

Because he served regularly as standby air ambulance pilot, a telephone bell was fixed to the chimney stack of his house so that he was always within earshot of a call even when in his garden — when the hotline rang it was often a source of great drama to the neighbours. In addition to the serious side of mercy flights on the air ambulance, Captain Starling recalls lighter moments too. Air sickness would occasionally overcome nurses and he remembers one patient, a country gentleman of the stiff upper lip variety, who insisted in maintaining his dignity and walking to the aircraft when a stretcher might have been more appropriate. The flight later passed through turbulence and the patient was then to be seen, still with complete composure, assisting the nurse whose head was on his lap. Our gentleman soothed her by stroking her hair with one hand while holding a strategically positioned sick bag in the other.

Upon another occasion a young relief doctor serving on Barra thought it might be prudent for a doctor to accompany a patient on the air ambulance flight in addition to the nurse already in attendance — who said that the opportunity for a free flight was the real motive? Anyway the poor doctor did not take to air travel at all and the nurse had to spend most of the time attending the ailing doctor, with the patient also pitching in to try and help relieve the unfortunate chap.

In May 1968 Captain Starling flew fifteen-year-old Alex Smith of Breasclete on the Isle of Lewis to Edinburgh. The youthful patient had inadvertently drunk the poisonous weedkiller paraquat from a lemonade bottle. Although it was not known at the time of the emergency flight, Alex was to become Europe's first lung transplant patient during the treatment that followed at Edinburgh Royal Infirmary.

From 1968 until his retirement in 1971 Captain Starling was Scottish Air Ambulance pilot and when he hung up his captain's cap in December 1971 he was the most Senior Captain of BEA. Captain Starling retired with only one unfulfilled ambition — despite having flown expectant mothers from island homes to city hospitals he never had an inflight birth.

Eric Starling commanded aircraft upon four occasions with members of the British Royal family on board. On one occasion his passengers were Princess Margaret and Lord Snowdon, and at another time he carried Prince Charles during the period when he was studying at Gordonstoun. Princess Alexandra was a passenger upon two occasions, once bound for Milan, and on the other Stockholm was the destination.

In retirement Captain Starling still enjoys frequent air travel, but as a passenger. And while he can look back on the old days with nostalgia Captain Starling also looks to the future and has an active interest in computers for which he writes his own programmes.

Robert McKean OBE FCIT

Robert McKean began a career in aviation as a Handley Page Hampden pilot with the Royal Air Force during the Second World War. His RAF career also saw him as an Instructor on Tiger Moth aircraft.

He was then seconded from the RAF to the British Overseas Airways Corporation and was appointed Staff Manager — Africa. From his base in Durban he assisted in the setting up of the "Horse Shoe" route around West Africa which BOAC flew with Shorts C-Class flying boats. With BOAC he was also to spend time in Rhodesia, Kenya, the Congo, India, Egypt and Spain.

When BEA was set up in 1947 he was one of the initial six staff based at Ruislip, joining on loan from BOAC as Staff Manager. In 1948 he moved to Renfrew where he assumed responsibility for co-ordinating the thirteen airports used by BEA in Scotland. These included the cockle strand on Barra where, upon the phasing out of the Rapides, De Havilland Herons were introduced specially fitted with a fixed tricycle under-carriage in order to withstand the extra stress imposed by the unusual landing surface there.

As the first Area Manager for BEA, he was also responsible for representing BOAC in Scotland in the early days. He later became General Manager of BEA's Scottish Division and finally, Director. When BEA Scottish Airways Division, Scotland's own airline within the BEA group, was set up in 1971 Mr McKean was appointed its Chairman.

He was active in many bodies involved in transportation in Scotland, including the Paisley and Glasgow Chambers of Commerce, the Scottish Tourist Board and the Scottish Section of the Institute of Transport of which he was Chairman. He served on the working party of the Highlands Transport Enquiry which produced the Cameron/Kilbrandon Report. In 1966 he was awarded the OBE.

Mr McKean had a particular interest in the Air Ambulance Service and assisted in the smooth handover from BEA to Loganair when Loganair was awarded the full Air Ambulance contract in 1973, the fortieth anniversary of the Scottish Air Ambulance; it was an opportune moment for him to produce a short history of the service.

Robert McKean retired from BEA on 30th June 1973 after a career of twenty-seven years with the airline.

Captain McIntosh steps back as Robert McKean christens the aircraft named in his honour
Photo by Randak Design and by courtesy of Hamish McKean

Chronology

1961   Capital Services (Aero) Ltd. starts up with Captain Duncan McIntosh as Chief Pilot.

1962   1st February — Loganair is formed as the aviation division of the Logan
       Construction Co Ltd.
    Piper Aztec and Piper Tripacer delivered.

1963   Second Piper Aztec and Piper Cherokee 180 boost the fleet to four aircraft.
    Army award contract to carry supplies to St Kilda.
    First scheduled service, between Dundee and Edinburgh, commences in October.
    Glasgow Flying Club is formed.

1964   Contract is awarded to carry newspapers to Stornoway.

1966   23rd January — Willie Logan is killed in air crash.
    Loganair becomes Loganair Ltd.
    Renfrew Airport is closed and head office is established at the new Glasgow
       Airport at Abbotsinch.
    First scheduled passengers are carried from Stornoway to Glasgow on the return
       leg of the newspaper run.

1967   First Britten-Norman Islander aircraft is delivered.
    Orkney inter-island scheduled services commence.
    Air Ambulance flights commence from Coll, Colonsay, Oronsay, Mull and Oban.

1968   Beech E18S joins the fleet.
    Glasgow—Oban—Mull route commences.
    8th October — Loganair Ltd is acquired by the National Commercial Bank of
       Scotland.

1969   Shorts Skyvan 3 joins the fleet.
    Glasgow—Aberdeen—Stavanger service commences.
    National Commercial Bank of Scotland merges with the Royal Bank of Scotland.

1970   Dundee—Glasgow service is inaugurated.
    First Shetland internal route, linking Sumburgh with Unst, is started.

1971   Eday is added to the Orkney inter-island network.
    The first Tingwall airstrip at Lerwick is opened.

1972   Fetlar and Whalsay are added to the Shetland internal network.
    Glasgow—Oban—Mull—Coll—Tiree seasonal service starts.
    Routes linking Inverness with Aberdeen, Dornoch, Wick and Skye, and
       linking Skye with Glasgow are launched.

1973   First Britten-Norman Trislanders join the fleet.
    Hoy is added to the Orkney inter-island network.
    First oil support contract, flying between Aberdeeen and Sumburgh, is
       awarded by Shell.
    Loganair is awarded the full Air Ambulance contract by the Scottish Home and
       Health Department.
    Loganair records its first in-flight birth with the arrival of Katy Devin
       on 2nd August above Kirkwall.

1974   Scheduled services are operated from Glasgow to Tiree and Barra.
    The world-wide 'oil crisis' — airline operating costs are increased drastically forcing
       proportionate increases in air fares.

1975   Inverness—Edinburgh route is inaugurated.

Western Isles inter-island service commences.

Beech E18S is gifted to the Royal Scottish Museum. Edinburgh (displayed at the Museum of Flight, East Fortune).

1976   Inverness—Wick—Kirkwall route is taken over from British Airways.

Fair Isle is added to the Shetland inter-island network.

1977   The first DHC Twin Otter is delivered.

Glasgow—Islay and Glasgow—Campbeltown routes are taken over from British Airways.

Flotta is added to the Orkney inter-island network.

1978   Scatsta is included in the Shetland internal network.

Glasgow—Mull direct service is started.

New terminal building is opened on 11th June at Barra Airport.

1979   First Shorts 330 is delivered.

Translink service to Prestwick is inaugurated.

Services started to Northern Ireland with a Glasgow—Londonderry route and a seasonal Glasgow—Enniskillen service.

Edinburgh—Lerwick route commences using DHC Twin Otter.

Chevron oil support contract, utilising up to seven aircraft, is commenced.

1980   Embraer Bandeirantes join the fleet.

Sumburgh base is closed and Shetland operations are centred at Tingwall Airport.

Edinburgh—Kirkwall route is launched using Shorts 330.

Seasonal service Prestwick—Isle of Man commences.

Edinburgh—Belfast trunk route is launched using Shorts 330.

1981   Route commences between Glasgow and Belfast.

First scheduled service to England with launch of Belfast—Blackpool route.

1982   Edinburgh—Manchester route is started with Shorts 330

Captain McIntosh retires in December after running Loganair for twenty-one years.

Scott Grier is new Managing Director.

1983   First Shorts 360 arrives.

Belfast Harbour Airport is opened.

Summer services from Londonderry to the Isle of Man and to Blackpool are started.

Fokker Friendship joins the fleet and operates the Edinburgh—Manchester service.

2nd December — Loganair is acquired by British Midland Airways.

1984   76-seat Vickers Viscount operates the Edinburgh—Manchester service during refurbishment of the Fokker Friendship.

Edinburgh—Inverness route is commenced.

Aberdeen base is closed.

Fokker Friendship operates a new Glasgow—Manchester route.

1985   Air Ambulance strips on Egilsay, Shapinsay and Wyre are brought on line.

1986   Monthly passenger carryings exceed twenty-five thousand for the first time.

Kirkwall—Fair Isle service is launched.

1987   Loganair celebrates its Silver Jubilee.

First Day Covers

Loganair has used another method of marking the milestones. New services have often been marked by the issuing of a special philatelic first day cover, a tradition established by the first airlines and continued by many today. The covers make fascinating mementos.

Above: First Day Cover carried on the inaugural mail flight of the Orkney Inter-Island Service which was operated in conjunction with the Orkney Isles Shipping Company.   *Below:* Captain Whitfield carried this special First Day Cover when flying the first scheduled flight to the airstrip he pioneered on the island of Fetlar

Flown on Loganair Flight LC 701
SUMBURGH - LERWICK (TINGWALL) - UNST
and then on Flight LC 702
UNST - FETLAR
the first scheduled flight to Fetlar
25th May, 1972
Aircraft   Britten-Norman BN2A Islander
Registration   G-AVRA
Pilot   Captain A. R. Whitfield
Total Flight Time   45 minutes
Carried by road to and posted in the
Fetlar Post Office for delivery to
Royal Air Force SAXA VORD

Capt. Whitfield   Capt. Whitfield
Loganair Ltd.   RAF Saxa Vord
                       Haroldswick

LOGANAIR LTD
WESTRAY TO PAPA WESTRAY

GUINNESS BOOK 21st Edition
OF RECORDS 31st OCTOBER 1974

The shortest scheduled flight in the world is that by Loganair between the Orkney Islands of Westray and Papa Westray which has been flown since September 1967. Though scheduled for 2 min.,in favourable wind conditions it is accomplished in 70 secs.

FLOWN IN BN 2A ISLANDER G-AWNR
FROM WESTRAY TO PAPA WESTWRAY
LOGANAIR FLIGHT No. LC 501
FLIGHT TIME: 69 seconds
PILOT: CAPT. ANDY ALSOP

ISLANDER STUDY GROUP,
POSTE RESTANTE,
Westray

Above: This First Day Cover was carried on the flight which gave Loganair a place in the Guinness Book of Records. Captain Andy Alsop later clipped the record to 58 seconds. For a time Loganair also claimed the world's second shortest scheduled service between Flotta and Hoy timetabled also at two minutes.
Below: One of the first scheduled services on which the DHC Twin Otter served was also the first Loganair service between Scotland and Northern Ireland.The route was Glasgow—Londonderry; the date 2 April 1979.

DHC 6 TWIN OTTER SERIES 300

AO 25

LOGANAIR
The Scottish Airline

SCOTLAND'S LONGEST ESTABLISHED
INDEPENDENT AIRLINE

OFFICIAL COVER

13ᴾ

Loganair Ltd.
First Scheduled Flight
Glasgow – Londonderry
2nd April 1979

Carried in DHC 6 Twin Otter 310 G-RBLA
Glasgow - Londonderry   2.4.79
Flight No: LC 401   Flight Time: 52 min.
Capt. K. E. Foster Capt. J. Taylor

A.P.P.
Cranbrook
Kent, U.K.

Air Ways

In the world of aviation change is constant. Throughout the world airline routes come and go as economic and political factors affect the needs of passengers and viability of routes for operators.

As will be seen from the following route maps, Loganair's network too has been constantly changing. Some services were ambitious experiments which nonethelesss did not attract sufficient public demand to justify their continuation, while others were important in their time until new factors, such as the construction of the Tay and Forth Road Bridges, the improvement of the A9 trunk road or the fast moving events of North Sea oil development, changed consumer requirements.

The overall trend has been progressive as the airline has grown from a few thin feeder routes, starting with the short hop from Dundee to Edinburgh which was operated in 1964, to what is now the most comprehensive domestic network in Britain.

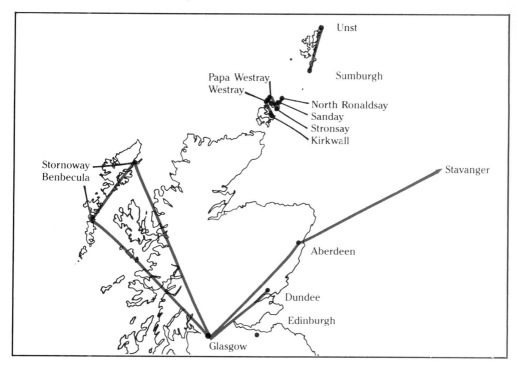

1970

The Orkney Isles network is already well established, while Unst is operational as the first step in the Shetland Isles internal service. Passengers were carried from Stornoway and Benbecula on the return leg of the newspaper run and Dundee had a link with Glasgow operating from Leuchars. The most ambitious route was the international service linking Glasgow and Aberdeen with Stavanger.

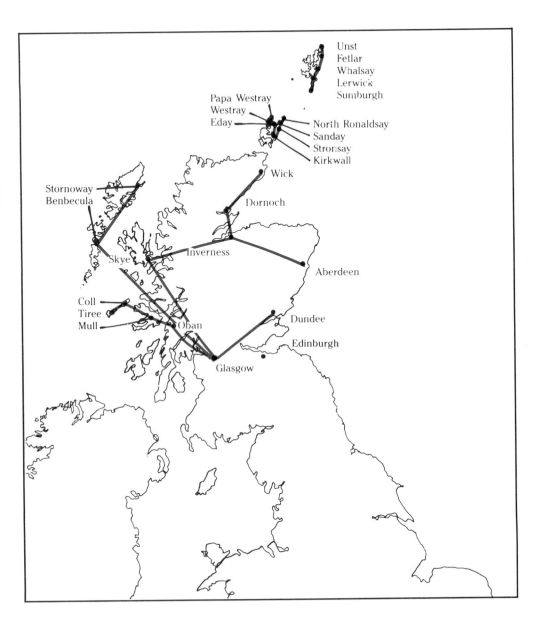

1972

The Stavanger service has been terminated but new services from Inverness are introduced to Aberdeen, Dornoch, Wick, and Skye which was also served from Glasgow. A Summer service to Oban, Mull, Coll and Tiree was inaugurated while the Shetlands internal network is now well developed.

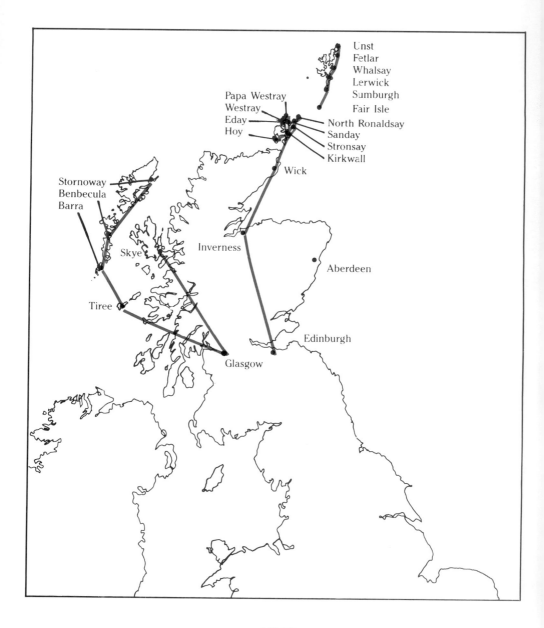

Unst
Fetlar
Whalsay
Lerwick
Sumburgh
Fair Isle

Papa Westray
Westray
Eday
Hoy
North Ronaldsay
Sanday
Stronsay
Kirkwall

Wick

Stornoway
Benbecula
Barra

Skye

Inverness

Aberdeen

Tiree

Edinburgh

Glasgow

1976

The network now includes services from Glasgow to Tiree and Barra. A Western Isles internal network also links Barra, Benbecula and Stornoway. Fair Isle joins the Shetland network and the southern Orkney island of Hoy is linked to Kirkwall now also served from Inverness and Wick. The Inverness—Edinburgh service is a main route for Loganair.

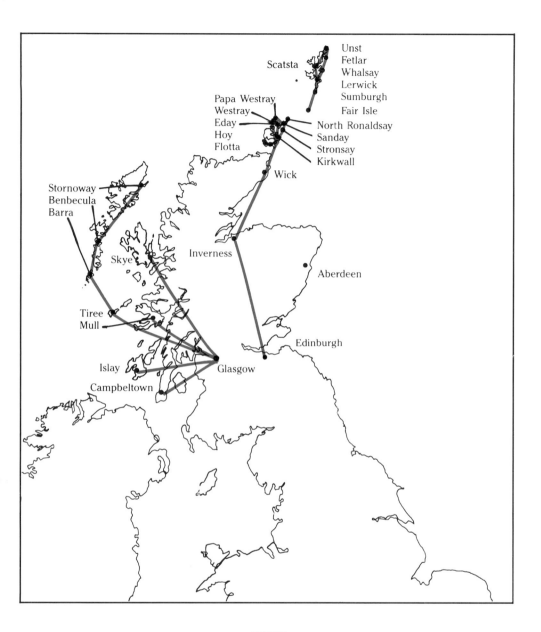

1978

Campbeltown and Islay are now also served from Glasgow and an attempt is again made to serve Mull, this time with a direct service from Glasgow. In the Shetlands a service is operated to Scatsta serving the Sullom Voe oil terminal, while the island of Flotta joined the Orkney network the previous year.

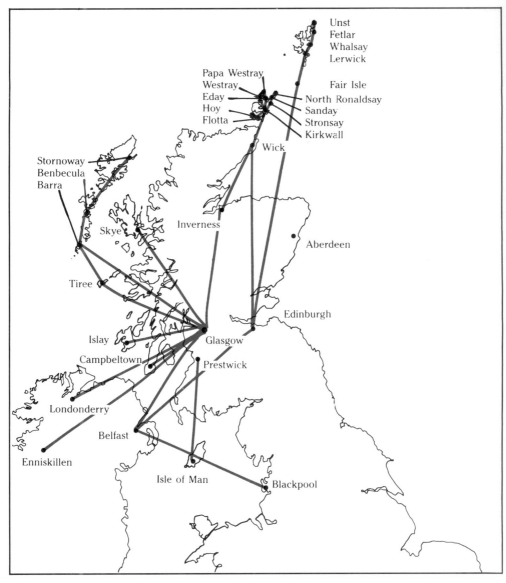

1981

The route map has expanded greatly. Northern Ireland has become an important new market with Belfast being served from Glasgow and Edinburgh, while Londonderry and Enniskillen are also served from Glasgow. The first service to England is also operated, but not from Scotland. The service to Blackpool is operated from Belfast. Inverness is now served from Glasgow.

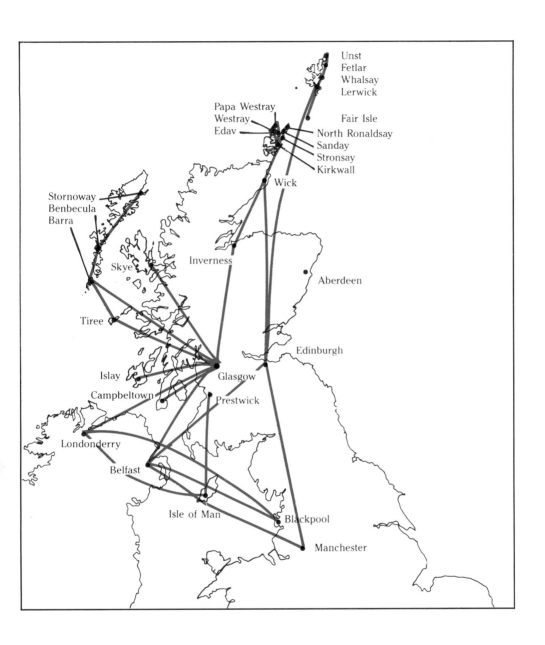

1983

Manchester is now an important destination with trunk routes from Edinburgh and Belfast. While Enniskillen has been dropped, Londonderry now has services to Blackpool and the Isle of Man.

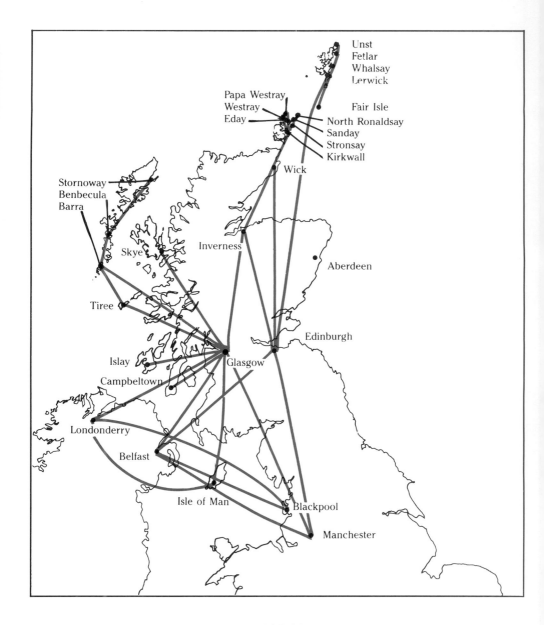

1985

Another important trunk route is added with the service between Glasgow and Manchester. The Edinburgh—Inverness route is in operation once more. Prestwick—Isle of Man has given way to the Glasgow—Isle of Man service which is promoted by Loganair on behalf of its operator, associate company Manx Airlines.

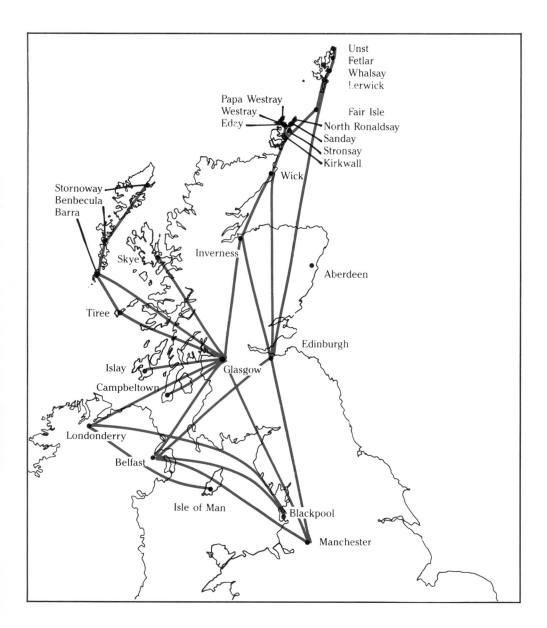

Unst
Fetlar
Whalsay
Lerwick

Papa Westray
Westray
Edey

Fair Isle
North Ronaldsay
Sanday
Stronsay
Kirkwall

Wick

Stornoway
Benbecula
Barra

Skye

Inverness

Aberdeen

Tiree

Islay

Glasgow

Edinburgh

Campbeltown

Londonderry

Belfast

Isle of Man

Blackpool

Manchester

1987

The Glasgow—Manchester route is now well established on the Loganair route map and
the double triangles linking Glasgow and Edinburgh with Belfast and Manchester are the
airline's trunk routes of the nineteen-eighties. Further north, Orkney and Shetland are now
linked via Fair Isle.

Fleet List

Aircraft Type	Reg. No.	Construction No.	Period of Operation				Notes
Piper PA23 Aztec 250A	G-ARMH	23-443	Del	1.62	Sold	7.65	
	G-ARHL	23-402	Lsd	11.64	Rtnd	12.64	leased from Aviation
			Lsd	5.66	Rtnd	8.66	Enterprises
Piper PA23 Aztec 250B	G-ASER	23-2282	Del	2.63	Sold	9.72	
	G-ASNA	23-2451	Lsd	6.69	Rtnd	7.69	leased from Aviation
							Enterprises
Piper PA23 Aztec 250C	G-ASYB	23-2641	Del	12.64	Sold	5.71	
	G-AWER	23-3852	Lsd	7.69	Rtnd	8.69	leased from CSE Aviation
Piper PA22 Tri-Pacer 160	G-ARHV	22-7614	Del	6.62	Sold	4.66	
Piper PA28 Cherokee 180	G-ASFL		Del	.63	Sold	10.65	
Piper PA32 Cherokee Six	G-ATJV	32-103	Del	12.65	Sold	3.68	
Bolkow Bo.208 Junior	G-ATRI	602	Del	4.66	w/o	8.70	Bought for Glasgow Flying Club. Written off at Balloch
Beech E18S	G-ASUG	BA-111	Del	5.68	Retd	3.75	Presented to Royal Scottish Museum. Ex N575C
Short SC.7 Skyvan 3	G-AWYG	1856	Del	3.69	Sold	12.73	Sold to USA
Britten-Norman BN2 Islander	G-ATWU	002	Lsd	7.67	Rtnd	8.67	leased from Britten-Norman in lieu of delivery following loss of prototype
	G-AVKC	004	Del	8.67	Sold	5.71	'Captain E E Fresson OBE'
	G-AVRA	006	Del	8.67	Sold	7.72	'Captain David Barclay MBE'
Britten-Norman BN2A Islander	G-AXKB	095	Del	8.69	Sold	6.78	'Sir James Young Simpson'
	G-AXFL	073	Lsd	9.70	Rtnd	12.70	leased from Glosair
	G-AXSS	R603	Del	3.71	Sold	5.79	'Robert McKean OBE FCIT'
	G-AWNR	030	Del	6.72	Sold	11.77	'Captain David Barclay MBE'
	G-AXRM	128	Lsd	8.72	Rtnd	4.73	leased fr. Humber Airways
	G-AXRN	129	Lsd	11.72	Rtnd	4.73	leased fr. Humber Airways
	G-AYXK	R659	Del	11.72	Sold	11.77	'Captain Eric A Starling FRMetS'
	G-AXVR	139	Del	1.73	Sold	11.77	'Captain E E Fresson OBE' from Aurigny Air Services
	G-BANL	318	Del	3.73			'Sister Jean Kennedy'
	G-AYCV	170	Lsd	11.73	Rtnd	4.74	leased fr. Cannon Aviation
	G-AYGL	R622	Lsd	12.73	Rtnd	1.74	leased from Shorelink
	G-BDDV	G461	Del	9.75	Sold	10.81	'E L Gandar Dower Esq' Sold to Olympic Airways
	G-BDVW	522	Del	11.77	w/o	6.84	'Sir James Young Simpson' Written off at Papa Westray
	G-BEDZ	544	Del	11.77			'Captain David Barclay MBE' changed to 'Captain Eric A Starling FRMetS'
	G-BEEG	550	Del	12.77			'Captain E E Fresson OBE' changed to 'Robert McKean OBE FCIT'
	G-BFCX	870	Del	4.79			'E L Gandar Dower Esq'
	G-BFNV	878	Del	4.79			'Captain David Barclay MBE OStJ'
	G-BJOP	2132	Del	9.84			'Captain E E Fresson OBE'

Aircraft Type	Reg. No.	Construction No.		Period of Operation		Notes
Britten-Norman	G-BAXD	359	Del	6.73	Sold 11.82	
Mk III-1 Trislander	G-BBNL	G350	Del	12.73	Sold 2.80	
	G-AZZM	321	Del	4.74	Sold 5.80	
	G-BCYC	G1011	Del	3.76	w/o 5.79	ex EL-AIB. W/o at Aberdeen
Britten-Norman	G-BDKR	G1020	Del	3.76	Sold 5.82	
Mk III-2 Trislander	G-BDOM	G1023	Del	6.76	Sold 12.82	
	G-BDOS	G1024	Del	11.76	Sold 4.82	
	G-BDTP	1028	Del	10.77	Sold 10.80	Sold to Sierra Leone Airways
DHC-6-310 Twin Otter	G-BELS	530	Del	1.77	Sold 3.82	Sold to Metropolitan Airways
	G-RBLA	578	Del	10.77	Sold 4.82	Sold to Express Airfreight
	VP-FAQ	347	Lsd	.78	Rtnd .80	Leased for summer periods fr. British Antarctic Survey
	VP-FAW	546	Lsd	.78	Rtnd .80	Leased for summer periods fr. British Antarctic Survey
	G-BGEN	616	Del	4.79		
	G-BGPC	635	Del	8.79	Sold 6.83	Sold to Nordic Oil, but leased back. Crashed on Islay 6.86
	G-BHFD	434	Del	11.79	Sold 3.82	Ex N26KA. Sold to Metropolitan Airways
	G-BEJP	525	Del	1.80		Bought from Mann Aviation
	G-BDHC	414	Lsd	3.80	Rtnd 9.80	Leased from Chubb
	G-BHXG	694	Del	7.80	Sold 8.85	
	G-BHTK	708	Del	9.80	Sold 8.85	
	G-BIEM	732	Del	12.80		
	G-BGMC	617	Lsd	11.85	Rtnd 10.86	Leased from Jersey European Airways
	SE-GEF G-BMXW	613	Lsd	4.86		Lsd as 300 series fr. Swedair. Converted to 310 series and put on British Register 10.86
Shorts 330	G-BGNA	SH3029	Del	3.79	Sold 3.83	
	G-BIRN	SH3067	Del	3.80	Sold 3.84	
Embraer Bandeirante EMB110P-2	G-BHHA	110244	Del	4.80	Sold 10.84	Sold to Provincetown Boston Airline. Re-registered N53PB
	G-BIBE	110288	Del	11.80	Sold 3.86	Sold to Jersey European Airways
Shorts 360	G-BKMX	SH3608	Del	3.83		
	G-BLGB	SH3641	Del	3.84		
	G-SALU	SH3628	Lsd	1.86	Rtnd 4.86	Lsd fr. Short Brothers Leasing
	G-BMLC	SH3688	Del	4.86		
	G-BMAR	SH3633	Lsd	10.86		Leased from Manx Airlines
Fokker Friendship 100	G-IOMA	10106	Lsd	11.83	Rtnd 5.86	Leased from British Midland
Fokker Friendship 200	G-BMAP	10302	Lsd	4.86		Leased from British Midland
Vickers Viscount 802	G-AOHM	162	Lsd	1.84	Rtnd 5.84	'The Flying Scotsman' leased from British Air Ferries

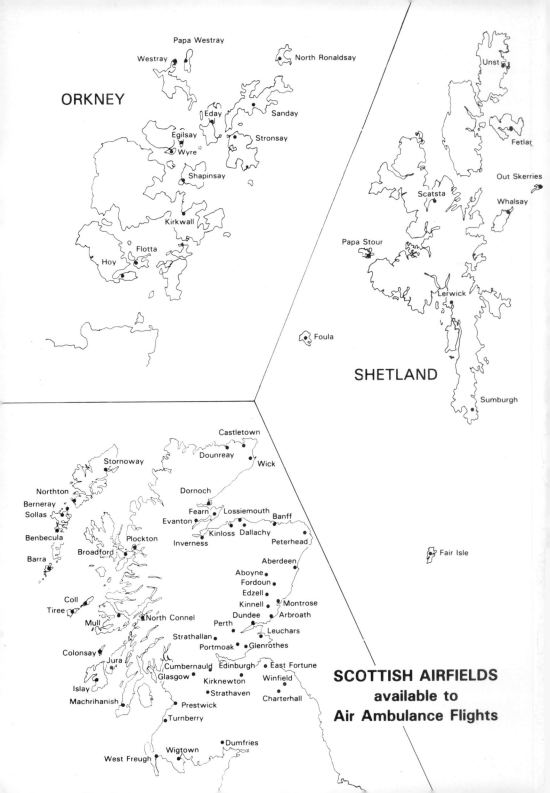

ORKNEY

Papa Westray
Westray
North Ronaldsay
Eday
Sanday
Egilsay
Stronsay
Wyre
Shapinsay
Kirkwall
Flotta
Hoy

SHETLAND

Unst
Fetlar
Out Skerries
Scatsta
Whalsay
Papa Stour
Lerwick
Foula
Sumburgh

Stornoway
Castletown
Northton
Dounreay
Wick
Berneray
Dornoch
Sollas
Fearn
Lossiemouth
Banff
Benbecula
Evanton
Dallachy
Plockton
Kinloss
Peterhead
Barra
Broadford
Inverness
Aberdeen
Aboyne
Fordoun
Edzell
Coll
Kinnell
Montrose
Tiree
North Connel
Dundee
Arbroath
Mull
Perth
Leuchars
Strathallan
Colonsay
Portmoak
Glenrothes
Jura
Cumbernauld
Edinburgh
East Fortune
Islay
Glasgow
Winfield
Kirknewton
Machrihanish
Strathaven
Charterhall
Prestwick
Turnberry
Dumfries
Wigtown
West Freugh

Fair Isle

SCOTTISH AIRFIELDS
available to
Air Ambulance Flights